THREE COSMIC
MESSAGES

Other Books by Mark Finley

10 Days in the Upper Room
The Church Triumphant
End-Time Hope
Fulfilling God's End-Time Mission (with Ernestine Finley)
Growing in Jesus, volumes 1 and 2
Hope for Trouble Times
Hope Beyond Tomorrow
Hope's End-Time Secrets (with Loron Wade)
Light Your World for God (with Ernestine Finley)
Making Friends for God
Persuasion
Revival for Mission
Revive Us Again
Studying Together
Understanding Daniel and Revelation
Understanding the Sanctuary
Unshakable Faith
What the Bible Says About

THREE COSMIC
MESSAGES

Mark Finley

Pacific Press®
Publishing Association

Nampa, Idaho | www.pacificpress.com

Hart Research Center

Cover design by Daniel Añez
Cover resources by Lars Justinen

Copyright © 2022 by Pacific Press® Publishing Association
Printed in the United States of America
All rights reserved

Originally published by Hart Research Center and adapted with permission
by Pacific Press® Publishing Association.

The author assumes full responsibility for the accuracy of all facts and quotations as
cited in this book.

Unless otherwise indicated, Scripture quotations are from the New King James Ver-
sion®. Copyright © 1982 by Thomas Nelson. Used by permission. All rights reserved.

Scripture quotations marked Phillips are from The New Testament in Modern English
by J. B. Phillips, copyright © 1960, 1972 J. B. Phillips. Administered by the Archbish-
ops' Council of the Church of England. Used by permission.

Purchase additional copies of this book by calling toll-free 1-800-765-6955 or by visit-
ing AdventistBookCenter.com.

ISBN 978-0-8163-6887-7

October 2022

Contents

Introduction

There is a conflict raging in the universe. It is all around us. We feel it deep within our hearts. Beyond what our eyes can see, there is a cosmic battle for control of the universe. It is a *Star Wars*–like intergalactic drama far more intriguing and thrilling than the award-winning movie. The throne of the universe is at stake. Will the forces of light triumph over the forces of darkness? Will right defeat wrong? Will Christ finally triumph over His archrival Satan? Will evil come to an end one day?

The prophecies of Revelation pull the curtain aside and give us a glimpse of this conflict. They reveal the climactic final events in this titanic struggle between the forces of righteousness and the forces of evil. Amazingly, God has sent three cosmic messages with divine urgency to prepare every person on planet Earth for what is coming. These urgent end-time messages come directly from God's heart of love. They reveal His last-day plans for our troubled planet. They carefully detail what is coming and how to prepare for the events that will soon burst upon this world as an overwhelming surprise.

Just look around you. The scene is being set. The threat of nuclear war is ever present. Even a limited nuclear war would kill millions and wreak environmental catastrophe on our planet. Climate change has become a grim reality. Many scientists are predicting severe consequences if something is not done soon. Our world's economy hangs by a slender thread, and a global monetary collapse may be just around the corner. Who knows when viruses now present will break out into the next pandemic, killing millions? And hunger and starvation are real threats in many parts of the world. Could it be that a political-religious alliance under the auspices of the antichrist will step forth one day as the solution to Earth's problems? Revelation has the answers.

In *Three Cosmic Messages*, I unfold Christ's last message of love to this planet, found in the heart of Revelation 14. You will thrill as you read these thought-provoking, hope-filled chapters. Each chapter is drenched in God's love as it candidly confronts the issues of our time from the perspective of Revelation's three prophetic cosmic messages. I pray that as you read these pages, you will be drawn closer to the Christ who made you, loves you with an everlasting love, and is soon coming to take you home.

1

Jesus Wins—Satan Loses

"And war broke out in heaven: Michael and his angels fought with the dragon; and the dragon and his angels fought, but they did not prevail, nor was a place found for them in heaven any longer. So the great dragon was cast out, that serpent of old, called the Devil and Satan, who deceives the whole world; he was cast to the earth, and his angels were cast out with him" (Revelation 12:7–9).

Episode 1: The war begins

Heaven! What a strange place for war! Was this first episode—the battle for the throne—a physical battle or simply a mental war game? It was both. Notice that every angel in heaven had to make a choice. There was no neutrality—no middle ground. Not one angel could say, "I do not want to participate. I think I will just be a bystander." Every angel had to make the all-important choice regarding whose side they would be on.

In Earth's final conflict, there is no neutrality. The messages from God's throne room, especially Revelation 14, are God's final messages to humanity. These messages lead us to choices that will decide our eternal destiny.

While there is no neutrality in Earth's final war, there is good news. Revelation 12 describes Christ's triumph in the galactic battle—the great controversy, which is the *Star Wars*–like conflict that began in heaven so long ago. In that battle, Jesus defeated Satan. Satan was cast out of heaven, and as Revelation 12:8 describes, the devil and his evil angels "did not prevail, nor was a place found for them in heaven any longer." In that battle for control of the universe, Jesus and His angels won, and the devil was defeated. Jesus has never lost a battle with Satan. In fact, His most significant victory occurred here on Earth, on a Friday at a place called Calvary. That was when and where the war was won!

In describing this cosmic war, Revelation 12:8 declares, "But they did not prevail." Notice this divine "but." There was war in heaven, but *Satan and his angels* did not prevail. In this first episode, Jesus, the Mighty Warrior, wins—and Satan loses. And His victory is ours.

Episode 2: Satan attacks Jesus

In the second episode of this cosmic drama, centuries pass, and Satan focuses his attention on destroying Jesus: "And the dragon stood before the woman who was ready to give birth, to devour her Child as soon as it was born. She bore a male Child who was to rule all nations with a rod of iron" (Revelation 12:4, 5).

In the Bible, a rod is a symbol of dominion or rulership. A rod of iron is a symbol of an unbreakable, all-powerful, and invincible rulership. Jesus faced every temptation that we experience and came through as Conqueror. Satan failed to destroy Him as a child, failed to defeat Him in His life, and failed to demolish Him in His death. The all-powerful risen Christ has defeated Satan.

As the apostle Paul puts it in Colossians 2:15: "Having disarmed principalities and powers, He made a public spectacle of them, triumphing over them in it [the cross]." The devil is a defeated foe. Christ has triumphed over him in His life, death, and resurrection. Since Jesus has already defeated the devil on Calvary's cross, we can be victorious too. How? By faith in what Christ has already done.

"Then I heard a loud voice saying in heaven, 'Now salvation, and strength, and the kingdom of our God, and the power of His Christ have come' " (Revelation 12:10). What has come? Salvation in Christ. Have you received it by faith? What has come? The strength and the power of His Christ. Have you received them by faith?

When we accept the righteousness of Christ as our righteousness, and we are declared righteous through His death, the dying Christ declares us righteous through His blood. The living Christ makes us righteous through His intercession.

Verse 11 states that believers "overcame him [Satan] by the blood of the Lamb and by the word of their testimony." Christ has overcome. Accept it. Believe it. Say it: Satan is a defeated foe!

Here is an eternal truth: Our faith grows as we accept Christ's victory as our own. Our own attitudes greatly affect our actions. Faith-filled Christians live in Christ's victory and thus triumph over the powers of hell. You will be victorious as you accept Christ's victory as your own, believe His victory is yours, focus on His strength and not your weakness, and speak out about His victory.

The devil suffered a deadly blow by Christ's death on the cross. Commenting on this victory, the apostle Paul declares, "For He [God] made Him who knew no sin to be sin for us, that we might become the righteousness of God in Him"(2 Corinthians 5:21). On the cross, Jesus bore the guilt, shame, and condemnation of our sins, taking away Satan's argument against us.

Christ's victory over Satan is complete, but the great controversy between Christ and Satan is not over yet. Satan was defeated in heaven and defeated at the cross, but he still wages war against the people of God on Earth. The apostle Paul puts it this way: "For we do not wrestle against flesh and blood, but against principalities, against powers, . . . in the heavenly places" (Ephesians 6:12).

The battle still rages, but victory for born-again believers is certain. This victory is described in Revelation 12:11: "And they overcame him by the blood of the Lamb and by the word of their testimony, and they did not love their lives to the death." The word "overcame" (*nikaó* in the original language of the Greek New Testament) can be literally translated "to conquer," "to prevail," "to triumph," or "to come through victoriously."

How is this possible? Revelation's answer is "by the blood of the Lamb" (verse 11).

The Lamb is a central figure in the book of Revelation. The Lamb of God, our perfect Savior, who gave His life in a perfect sacrifice, is mentioned twenty-eight times in the book of Revelation.

In the book of Revelation, numbers are significant. In Revelation, seven is a symbol of perfection. Four is a symbol of universality. It represents the four points of the compass—north, south, east, and west. Let us look at just one of these twenty-eight passages and catch a glimpse of the majesty of this symbolism of the Lamb. Consider Revelation 5:6: "And I looked, and behold, in the midst of the throne and of the four living creatures, and in the midst of the elders, stood a Lamb as though it had been slain, having seven horns and seven eyes, which are the seven Spirits of God sent out into all the earth."

The Lamb is a symbol of sacrifice. Remember when John the Baptist, seeing Jesus, declared, "Behold! The Lamb of God who takes away the sin of the world!" (John 1:29)? Through His sacrifice, our guilt is gone, our sins are forgiven, and we are no longer condemned for our transgressions. They are taken away from us. He bears the guilt, the shame, and the condemnation of our sins.

When we accept in faith what Christ has done for us, our debt is canceled, and our sins are forgiven. If we are forgiven, there is nothing that we can be accused of. If you have come to Christ, accepted His sacrifice on the cross, and are His child, your place in heaven has already been assured through His victory! "But God . . . raised us up together, and made us sit together in the heavenly places in Christ Jesus" (Ephesians 2:4, 6).

These verses show that there is a great bond between Christ and His people. We are united with Him in His death, are raised with Him in His resurrection, and are seated with Him in heavenly places in His exaltation. When we are united with Christ, His death for sin assures us that we do not have to die for our sins. Because we were united with Christ when He rose again and ascended into heaven, we have a status in heaven.

Heaven is our true home. We Christians have a right to it. We have a certain status there as God's children. Through Jesus, because of His death, we have the right—the guarantee—of eternity. Satan is a defeated foe. The stranglehold of death is broken. By faith, through the blood of Christ, eternity is ours. No matter how contrary it may seem in today's troubled world, Satan is a defeated foe.

Satan's charge against God in heaven was that He was a dictator—a tyrant who did not have the best interest of His creatures in view. The Cross defeats that argument and reveals a God of infinite love who will do anything to save us. Love triumphs over hate.

Napoleon is said to have made this insightful statement: "Alexander, Caesar, Charlemagne, and myself have founded empires. But upon what did we rest the creations of our genius? Upon *force*! Jesus Christ alone founded his empire upon love; and at this moment millions of men would die for him."[1]

Episode 3: Satan attacks God's people in the Middle Ages

After Calvary, the Christian church was established and immediately became Satan's target. "Now when the dragon saw that he had been cast to the earth, he persecuted the woman who gave birth to the male Child. But the woman was given two wings of a great eagle, that she might fly into the wilderness to her place, where she is nourished for a time and times and half a time, from the presence of the serpent" (Revelation 12:13, 14). Earlier in the chapter, John declares, "The women fled into the wilderness, where she has a place prepared by God, that they should feed her there one thousand two hundred and sixty days" (verse 6).

Please notice these phrases: "a place prepared by God" (verse 6); "her place, where she is nourished" (verse 14); and "the earth helped the woman" (verse 16). Every time the devil attacks a child of God, God provides a place of refuge for His children.

Bible prophecy often uses code words. It speaks of strange beasts, mystic symbols, and unusual signs. The good news is that the same God who revealed this prophetic symbolism provides the keys to unlock those mysteries in His Word.

When a prophecy is symbolic, its periods are symbolic. Here are two Old Testament passages that help us more clearly understand the 1,260 days—time, times, and half a time—when the woman (the church) escaped to the wilderness. In Numbers 14:34, we read, "According to the number of the days in which you spied out the land, forty days, for each day you shall bear your guilt one year, namely forty years."

Twelve Israelite spies visited the land of Canaan for forty days. Ten of them returned with a negative report. God's prophetic word declared that for each day they spied out the land, the Israelites would wander in the wilderness for one year. As predicted, the Israelites wandered in the wilderness for forty years. This helps to establish in Scripture what is known as the day-year principle. Each prophetic day equals one literal year. We find this principle delineated in other places in the Bible. Ezekiel 4:6 says of God's judgment on His people: "I have laid on you a day for each year." In Genesis 29:27, Laban commands Jacob to labor for Rachel for a week—or seven years. One of the great confirmations of Bible prophecy is that when the day-year principle is applied, it fits the historical events described by the prophecy perfectly.

Back to Revelation 12 now. Here we find the prediction that the people of God would be persecuted for 1,260 prophetic days—or literal years. History records that during the Middle Ages, the medieval church united with the political powers of the state from AD 538 to AD 1798, and this persecution occurred. Those who did not conform to the popular religious teachings of this church-state union were oppressed and persecuted. They were often hunted, and some were martyred. Like the apostle Paul, they could say, "We are hard-pressed on every side, yet not crushed; we are perplexed, but not in despair; persecuted, but not forsaken; struck down, but not destroyed" (2 Corinthians 4:8, 9).

But at the end of the 1,260-year prophecy in 1798, General Berthier led the armies of France into Rome and captured Pope Pius VI, who later died in captivity. Inquisitions no longer threatened those who believed in Scripture alone as their spiritual authority. It all happened as Revelation had foretold!

Victory is ours, not because there are no struggles or battles to fight but because Christ is already Victor through His life, death, glorious resurrection, and ministry in the heavenly sanctuary. And soon, very soon, Satan will be vanquished forever. We are still in the battle, but the victory has already been won.

One religious writer uses this wonderful illustration:

Imagine a city under siege. The enemy that surrounds the city will not let anyone or anything enter or leave. Supplies are running low, and the citizens are fearful.

But in the dark of the night, a spy sneaks through the enemy lines. He has rushed to the city to tell the people that in another place the main enemy force has been defeated; the leaders have already surrendered. The people do not need to be afraid. It is only a matter of time until the besieging troops receive the news and lay down their weapons.[2]

Similarly, the enemy has been defeated at Calvary. Things are not the way they seem to be. It is only a matter of time until it becomes clear to all that the battle is over. Christ has called us to victory, not defeat, and triumph, not loss.

Episode 4: Satan attacks the remnant

There is one last episode in the story of Revelation 12: "And the dragon was enraged with the woman, and he went to make war with the rest of her offspring, who keep the commandments of God and have the testimony of Jesus" (verse 17). The dragon—that is, Satan—is angry with the woman, who is God's church. He is furious with a people who keep the commandments of God, and he will do everything he can to destroy them.

Eventually, he instigates a decree so that they cannot buy or sell. If they do not comply, they will be threatened with imprisonment, torture, and even death. Earth's last war is not centered on the Middle East; it is focused on the minds of God's people. It is a battle between two opposing forces—the forces of heaven and the forces of hell.

The central questions in this final war are, Who has our loyalty? Where is our allegiance? Heaven calls for a final generation of believers who are so charmed by Christ's love, redeemed by His grace, committed to His purposes, empowered by His Spirit, and obedient to His commands that they are willing to face death for His cause.

Our world is headed for a major crisis. We are on a collision course. But here is the incredibly good news: we are on the winning side. Christ and His church will triumph. In Jesus, by Jesus, through Jesus, and because of Jesus, we will triumph at last. Christ's victory is the eternal guarantee of our victory. Our heavenly High Priest will never let us down. He will get His people through Earth's last hours.

---

1. John S. C. Abbott, *The History of Napoleon Bonaparte*, vol. 1 (New York: Harper & Brothers, 1855), 246; emphasis in the original.

2. Richard J. Mouw, *Uncommon Decency*, rev. ed. (Downers Grove, IL: InterVarsity, 2010), 163.

2

A Movement of Destiny

God is never caught by surprise. In these last days of human history, He has sent a special message designed to meet the need of the hour. Revelation pictures this message as being carried by three angels in the midst of heaven, flying with their urgent, end-time message to the ends of the earth. Revelation's message invites all humans to make their eternal choice. This is a moment of destiny—a moment of decision.

As James Russell Lowell put it in his poem "The Present Crisis": "Once to every man and nation comes the moment to decide, / In the strife of Truth with Falsehood, for the good or evil side."[1]

Our world is at a crossroads. This is a moment of destiny; each one of us is making crucial decisions every day. Character is not formed in an instant. It is the result of a lifetime of daily decisions. As the Holy Spirit impresses our minds, as we yield daily to His impressions and allow our characters to be molded by the grace of Christ, we become more like Jesus day by day. Revelation's message is Jesus' final message of mercy to lead us from trusting in our own goodness and righteousness to living by faith and trusting in His grace. There will come a day when every human being on planet Earth will have made their final, irrevocable decision. Revelation's message of Christ's righteousness, which delivers us from the bondage of guilt and the grip of sin in our lives, will echo and re-echo throughout the earth. The day will finally come when the words of Christ will be fulfilled: "And this gospel of the kingdom will be preached in all the world as a witness to all the nations, and then the end will come" (Matthew 24:14).

Eternal choices

In Revelation 14:6–20, six angels are mentioned. The first three angels announce the final judgment. The first angel announces that the hour of God's judgment has come. The second angel announces judgment on Babylon, the apostate religious powers of our day. The third angel announces judgment on the beast who oppresses, persecutes, and declares war on the people of God.

The last three angels execute the judgment announced by the first three angels. The Son of man is in the center of these six angels, in triumph over the powers of hell, to deliver His people.

The last part of Revelation 14 describes the execution of Heaven's final judgment (verses 14–20). "Then I looked, and behold, a white cloud, and on the cloud sat One like the Son of Man, having on His head a golden crown, and in His hand a sharp sickle" (verse 14).

You may recall that when Jesus ascended to heaven, Luke recorded that the wondering disciples stood gazing up into heaven, and "while they watched, He [Jesus] was taken up, and a cloud received Him out of their sight" (Acts 1:9). Two angels then declared to the amazed disciples, "Men of Galilee, why do you stand gazing up into heaven? This same Jesus, who was taken up from you into heaven, will so come in like manner as you saw Him go into heaven" (verse 11).

Three Cosmic Messages

Revelation 14:14 is the fulfillment of Acts 1:11. Jesus ascended in a cloud of angels and will return with a cloud of angels. Notice the expression Scripture uses to describe Jesus in Revelation 14:14: "Then I looked, and behold, a white cloud, and on the cloud sat One like the *Son of Man*" (emphasis added).

Jesus is "the Son of Man." This was His favorite title, which He used for Himself. It is used eighty-two times in the Gospels alone. (Matthew uses it thirty times.) It is often used in connection with the second coming of Christ.

Consider the following three Bible passages:

"For the Son of Man will come in the glory of His Father with His angels, and then He will reward each according to his works" (Matthew 16:27).

"For as the lightning comes from the east and flashes to the west, so also will the coming of the Son of Man be. . . .

". . . Then the sign of the Son of Man will appear in heaven, and then all the tribes of the earth will mourn, and they will see the Son of Man coming on the clouds of heaven with power and great glory" (Matthew 24:27, 30).

"When the Son of Man comes in His glory, and all the holy angels with Him, then He will sit on the throne of His glory" (Matthew 25:31).

Notice the three elements in each of these passages: (1) Jesus is coming; (2) He will execute judgment when He comes; and (3) the destiny of the nations and all humanity will be decided for eternity.

The Son of man is also mentioned in the light of the judgment in

Daniel 7:9, 10, 13, 14. In verses 9 and 10, Daniel views the seating of the heavenly court with ten thousand times ten thousand angelic, heavenly beings gathered around the throne. The judgment is set, and the books—the celestial records of our lives—are opened before the universe.

"I watched till thrones were put in place,
And the Ancient of Days was seated;
His garment was white as snow,
And the hair of His head was like pure wool.
His throne was a fiery flame,
Its wheels a burning fire" (verse 9).

In verses 13 and 14, the Son of man approaches the Ancient of Days, the Father, and receives His eternal kingdom. The judgment reveals before the entire universe that the Father, Son, and Holy Spirit—the divine heavenly trio—have done everything possible to save all humanity.

"Then to Him was given dominion and glory and a kingdom,
That all peoples, nations, and languages should serve Him.
His dominion is an everlasting dominion,
Which shall not pass away,
And His kingdom the one
Which shall not be destroyed" (verse 14).

In the judgment, the records of our lives are opened. The choices we have made are revealed. The question in the judgment is not good deeds weighed against bad deeds; rather, it is, What have we done with Jesus? What have our daily choices been in relation to Him? Have we responded to His grace? Have we accepted His loving sacrifice on Calvary's cross? Has our response to His grace, prompted by His Spirit, made a difference in our lives?

Jesus unfolds before millions of heavenly beings that His sinless life was enough. His perfect sacrifice was enough. His atoning death was enough.

The victor's crown

In Revelation 14, John describes Jesus as "the Son of Man, having on His head a golden crown, and in His hand a sharp sickle" (verse 14). Notice what He wears on His head when He returns to reap Earth's final harvest. The Greek word for "crown" is *stephanos*. It is a victor's crown. When an athlete won an important contest, he or she was given a *stephanos*—a victor's crown. It was a crown of honor. It was a crown of glory. It was a crown symbolizing victory.

Jesus once wore a crown of thorns, symbolizing shame and mockery. He was once despised and rejected by men. He was once reviled, ridiculed, spat upon, beaten, and whipped. But now He wears the crown of glory. He comes as King of kings and Lord of lords. Notice what the fourth angel says. "And another angel came out of the temple, crying with a loud voice to Him who sat on the cloud, 'Thrust in Your sickle and reap, for the time has come for You to reap, for the harvest of the earth is ripe' " (verse 15).

Where does the fourth angel come from? The angel comes from the presence of God in the glory of the temple. God looks at the angel and says, "It is time. The harvest is fully ripe." The angel flies from the temple to Jesus and declares with a loud voice: "It is time. The harvest is ripe, Jesus. Go! Marshal the forces of heaven. Command the angels! Go and get Your children, and bring them home. The long night of Earth is over. Their suffering is finished. They have been faithful."

Another harvest

In Revelation 14:17–20, there is another harvest—the bloody harvest of unholy grapes. Both harvests are fully ripe. The harvest of golden grain represents the deliverance of the righteous.

> And another angel came out from the altar, who had power over fire, and he cried with a loud cry to him who had the sharp sickle, saying, "Thrust in your sharp sickle and gather the clusters of the vine of the earth, for her grapes are fully ripe." So the angel thrust his sickle into the earth and gathered the vine of the earth, and threw it into the great winepress of the wrath of God. And the winepress was trampled outside the city, and blood came out of the winepress, up to the horses' bridles, for one thousand six hundred furlongs (verses 18–20).

"Another angel came out from the altar, who had power over fire": here is the angel who commands the fires of God's final judgment. The harvest is ripe. Sin has reached its limits. Rebellion has crossed the line of God's mercy. A loving God has done everything He can do. There is nothing more grace can do to redeem those who have repeatedly rejected the claims of His Holy Spirit.

Throughout Scripture, God's wrath is His judgment on sin. The time has come to execute God's final judgment on sin and make an utter end of rebellion. Some have wondered what the text means when it declares that "blood came out of the winepress, up to the horses' bridles, for one thousand six hundred furlongs."

One thousand six hundred furlongs is about 184 miles. That is approximately the length of Israel from north to south. The imagery is clear. The destruction of evil will be complete. There will not be one vestige of sin left in the land. There will not be a trace of evil. Sin will be finally, completely blotted out forever.

Here is the urgent prophetic message of Revelation 14. Every seed is ready to harvest. The grain is fully ripe, and the grapes are fully ripe. The people of God reveal His image of grace, compassion, mercy, and love before the universe. The children of the evil one reveal greed, lust, hate, jealousy, and impurity. The character of Jesus is revealed in one group, and the character of Satan in the other.

Sowing and reaping

In the last days, the seeds of righteousness and the seeds of wickedness will be fully ripe. Every one of us is sowing and growing seeds in the choices we make day by day. What seeds are you sowing? The fruit we produce in our lives is the result of the seeds we sow.

You cannot sow the seeds of evil and reap righteousness. You cannot sow the seeds of immorality and reap purity. You cannot sow the seeds of dishonesty and reap honesty. You cannot sow the seeds of worldliness and reap heavenly-mindedness. You cannot sow the seeds of anger and reap patience. You cannot sow the seeds of intemperance and reap health. You cannot sow the seeds of the world's mass media entertainment and reap Heaven's character. Ellen White notes, "The mind gradually adapts itself to the subjects upon which it is allowed to dwell."[2]

What does the mind do? It gradually adapts itself to the subjects it is allowed to dwell on. Subtly, imperceptibly, almost unnoticed at first, our characters and personalities change based on the seeds we are sowing in our minds. Sow good seeds, and you will produce good fruit. Sow the evil seeds of this world, and you will produce the fruit of this world in your character.

Every harvest has distinct and specific laws of sowing and reaping. This is true in the natural world and in the spiritual world. "Do not be deceived, God is not mocked; for whatever a man sows, that he will also reap" (Galatians 6:7).

Notice the expression "God is not mocked." The word for "mocked" comes from the Greek word *muktḗr*—the nose. It means "to turn up the nose at," "to treat with contempt," or "to ridicule." We cannot ignore God's Word, His truth, His laws, and His eternal heavenly principles and treat them with contempt without experiencing the consequences in our own lives and characters.

Notice the next phrase in our text: "God is not mocked; for whatever a man sows, that he will also reap." The word "whatever" makes this law of sowing and reaping universal—it applies to anything and everything we sow. Sow good seeds, and you will have positive results. Sow evil seed, and you will have negative results.

Since everything reproduces after its kind, God can never be mocked. Just as no one can sow beans and produce watermelons or breed cows and produce Thoroughbred horses, no one can sow evil seeds and produce a good crop. We cannot sow discord and produce unity. We cannot sow lies and produce truth. We cannot sow sin and produce holiness. We cannot sow unrighteousness and produce righteousness. We cannot sow intemperance and produce health. We cannot sow criticism of others and produce positive relationships with them. We cannot sow prayerlessness and produce godliness. We cannot sow a life without Bible study and produce depths of spiritual character.

If we sow indifference to God and spiritual values and priorities, we reap the fruit of indifference—apathy, spiritual complacency, and frustration in our spiritual lives. Here is something for us to think about: sow a *thought*, reap an *act*; sow an *act*, reap a *habit*; sow a *habit*, reap a *character*; sow a *character*, reap a *destiny*.

The promise and warning of Scripture are that we reap what we sow. This means that life's choices are filled with good and bad consequences—both temporal and eternal. Christians often make two fatal mistakes regarding this law of sowing and reaping. The first is spending time grieving over the seeds they sowed in past years. Their past mistakes, failures, and sins haunt them. Second, they worry that the seeds they have already sown will ruin their future lives of joy and fruitfulness in God's cause. They have the idea that their past shapes their future.

Only when you and I live in the joy of Christ's presence and the delight of His salvation can our lives be filled with the abundant life He offers. If we live in the guilt of yesterday and the worries of tomorrow, we will certainly be discouraged.

Will you choose today to respond daily to the wooing of God's Spirit, live in the joy of His grace, and rejoice that we have a Savior who has done, is doing, and will do everything possible to save us? We are sowing seeds for the final harvest. Jesus is coming again, and He longs to take you home to live with Him forever.

---

1. James Russell Lowell, "The Present Crisis," in *Poems*, 2nd ser. (Boston: B. B. Mussey, 1848), 55.

2. Ellen G. White, *The Great Controversy* (Nampa, ID: Pacific Press®, 2002), 555.

5

The Everlasting Gospel

For Seventh-day Adventists, the three angels' messages in Revelation 14 are our rallying point. They are our identifying statements of faith. They define who we are as a people and describe our mission to the world. We find our unique prophetic identity outlined in Revelation 14:6–12, and it is here that we find our passion for proclaiming the gospel to the entire world.

Ellen White puts it this way: "In a special sense Seventh-day Adventists have been set in the world as watchmen and light-bearers. To them has been entrusted the last warning for a perishing world. On them is shining wonderful light from the Word of God. They have been given a work of the most solemn import—the proclamation of the first, second, and third angels' messages. There is no other work of so great importance. They are to allow nothing else to absorb their attention."[1]

A grace-filled book of hope
When most people think about the Bible's last book, Revelation,

they do not think about grace. Their thoughts immediately turn to frightening beasts, mystic symbols, and strange images. The book upsets many people. On one occasion, a barber commented to an Adventist pastor, "I read the book of Revelation last evening and became so frightened that it was difficult to sleep." Thankfully, the pastor was able to reassure him that the message of Revelation is one of hope.

It is unfortunate that so many people are hesitant to read Revelation and that they view it through the eyes of fear. The first verse of the first chapter proclaims the book as the Revelation of Jesus Christ: "The Revelation of Jesus Christ, which God gave Him to show His servants—things which must shortly take place" (Revelation 1:1).

Revelation is a grace-filled message of end-time hope. It describes Christ as the slain Lamb twenty-eight times. It tells us in Revelation 1:5 that He is the One "who loved us and washed us from our sins in His own blood." It proclaims that in Christ, we are forgiven. Grace pardons our past, empowers our present, and provides hope for our future. In Christ, we are delivered from sin's penalty and power, and one day soon, we will be delivered from its presence. This is the hope- and grace-filled message of the Bible's last book.

The eternal gospel

Notice that the three angels' messages of Revelation 14 begin with the eternal or "everlasting gospel" (verse 6). The gospel is the foundation stone upon which Revelation's messages rest. If we fail to understand the depth of the gospel, we will miss the entire point of the three angels' messages. We can never fully understand the issues in God's judgment-hour message if we do not understand the gospel. We will never fully understand Heaven's warning about the fall of Babylon and God's call for His people to come out of Babylon if we fail to understand the gospel. We will never understand the fateful warning about the mark of the beast if we fail to understand the gospel.

What is the gospel? Theologians have discussed this question for centuries. Maybe our clearest answer can be found at Calvary. A few feet from where Jesus hung on the cross, a convicted thief was also being crucified. The pain of crucifixion was terrible—hand-forged spikes flattened the median nerve that runs through the arm, wrist, and hand. If you have ever bumped your elbow against a hard surface, you know that the nerves in the arms and hands are sensitive. But in crucifixion, there was more than a momentary jolt of pain. The head of an iron spike pierced the nerve, and the pain continued without relief. Crucified victims usually responded with screams and curses, and the thief did exactly that. For a time, he even cursed Jesus. But then he heard Jesus react to the same pain, not with a curse but with a prayer for forgiveness.

Something awakened in his mind—perhaps his early boyhood memories of reciting the Shema at bedtime or perhaps a Torah extract he had heard at the synagogue, revealing Israel's suffering Messiah. And then he did three remarkable things.

First, he accepted his own guilt; he acknowledged that he was a sinner. Then he accepted the righteousness of Christ. And finally, having confessed that he did not deserve salvation, he asked for it anyway—and got it, an assurance direct from the Lord Himself!

That is the elegant simplicity of Calvary. That is the heart of the gospel. On the cross, Christ took the initiative. With outstretched arms, He reached out to lost humanity. The dying thief saw God's love revealed in the crucified Christ. We acknowledge our own mistakes, we acknowledge the righteousness of Christ, and then, based on His righteousness alone, we accept the salvation He so freely offers.

In his letter to the church at Corinth, Paul describes the gospel eloquently.

Moreover, brethren, I declare to you the gospel which I preached to you, which also you received and in which you stand. . . .

For I delivered to you first of all that which I also received: that Christ died for our sins according to the Scriptures, and that He was buried, and that He rose again the third day according to the Scriptures, and that He was seen by Cephas [Peter], then by the twelve (1 Corinthians 15:1, 3–5).

Paul is clear in his definition of the gospel. The gospel is the incredibly good news of Christ's death for our sins, His glorious resurrection, and His ever-present love and concern for us.

The gospel is the joyous reality that Jesus will deliver us from sin's penalty and power—and finally, from its very presence. By faith in His shed blood and resurrection power, we are delivered from the guilt and the grip of sin. "Being justified freely by His grace through the redemption that is in Christ Jesus, whom God set forth as a propitiation by His blood, through faith, to demonstrate His righteousness, because in His forbearance God had passed over the sins that were previously committed, to demonstrate at the present time His righteousness, that He might be just and the justifier of the one who has faith in Jesus" (Romans 3:24–26).

The crucified Christ redeemed him from the condemnation and guilt of his past.[2] The resurrected Christ gave him power for the present. And the returning Christ gave him hope for the future. Notice three points in this passage: (1) we are justified freely by grace; (2) grace is a declaration of God's righteousness; and (3) through grace, God justifies those who believe in Jesus.

In Romans 5:6–8, Paul reviews the concept of grace: "For when we were still without strength, in due time Christ died for the ungodly. For scarcely for a righteous man will one die; yet perhaps for a good man someone would even dare to die. But God demonstrates His own love toward us, in that while we were still sinners, Christ died for us."

Christ's grace is unmerited, undeserved, and unearned. Jesus died the agonizing, painful death that lost sinners will die. He experienced the fullness of the Father's wrath or judgment against sin. He was rejected so we could be accepted. He died the death that was ours so we could live the life that was His. He wore the crown of thorns so we could wear a crown of glory. He was nailed upright in torturous pain upon a cross so we could sit upright on a heavenly throne with the redeemed of all ages, wearing the robes of royalty forever. Marvel of all marvels, wonder of all wonders, in our shame and guilt, Jesus did not reject us—He reached out in love to accept us.

Ellen White explains the significance of the Cross in *The Desire of Ages.*

Upon Christ as our substitute and surety was laid the iniquity of us all. He was counted a transgressor, that He might redeem us from the condemnation of the law. The guilt of every descendant of Adam was pressing upon His heart. The wrath of God against sin, the terrible manifestation of His displeasure because of iniquity, filled the soul of His Son with consternation. All His life Christ had been publishing to a fallen world the good news of the Father's mercy and pardoning love. Salvation for the chief of sinners was His theme. But now with the terrible weight of guilt He bears, He cannot see the Father's reconciling face. The withdrawal of the divine countenance from the Saviour in this hour of supreme anguish pierced His heart with a sorrow that can never be fully understood by man. So great was this agony that His physical pain was hardly felt.

Satan with his fierce temptations wrung the heart of Jesus. The Saviour could not see through the portals of the tomb. Hope did not present to Him His coming forth from the grave a

31

conqueror, or tell Him of the Father's acceptance of the sacrifice. He feared that sin was so offensive to God that Their separation was to be eternal. Christ felt the anguish which the sinner will feel when mercy shall no longer plead for the guilty race. It was the sense of sin, bringing the Father's wrath upon Him as man's substitute, that made the cup He drank so bitter, and broke the heart of the Son of God.[3]

On the cross, Christ assumed the penalty for sin for all humanity. He bore the guilt and shame of sin for the entire human race. The dark shadows of death hung over the cross, and Jesus experienced the death that all unrepentant sinners will die as a result of the guilt and shame of sin (Galatians 3:13; 2 Corinthians 5:21).

This is the story of a Savior's love beyond measure. This is the story of a Savior who loves us so much that He would rather experience hell itself than have one of us be lost. This is the story of a boundless, unfathomable, incomprehensible, undying, unending, and infinite love that longs for us to be with Him eternally and the One who was willing to assume the guilt, condemnation, and consequences of our sin and, if need be, stay separated from His Father forever, if that is what it took to save us.

Redeemed by grace, motivated by love, and empowered by Christ's Spirit, who dwells in our hearts by faith, sin no longer reigns in our lives (see Romans 6:12). Although, in our humanness, we may fail at times, we are no longer under the domain of sin. Its hold on us has been broken. According to Romans 8:15, the apostle Paul says, "For you did not receive the spirit of bondage again to fear, but you received the Spirit of adoption by whom we cry out, 'Abba, Father.' "

The story of grace
Grace is not an afterthought. God is never caught by surprise. He is not subject to the changing winds of humanity's choices. His plan

to deliver us from the domain of sin was not an afterthought when sin reared its ugly head. John speaks of the "Lamb slain from the foundation of the world" (Revelation 13:8). The apostle Peter adds, "You were not redeemed with corruptible things, like silver or gold, from your aimless conduct received by tradition from your fathers, but with the precious blood of Christ, as of a lamb without blemish and without spot. He indeed was foreordained before the foundation of the world, but was manifest in these last times for you" (1 Peter 1:18–20).

The phrase "everlasting gospel" in Revelation 14:6 speaks of the past, the present, and the future. When God created humanity with the capacity to make moral choices, He anticipated that humans could make errant choices. Once His creatures had the capacity to choose, they had the capacity to rebel against His loving nature.

The only way to avoid this reality would have been to create robotic beings, controlled and manipulated by some divine cosmic plan. Forced allegiance is contrary to God's very nature. Love requires choice, and once beings were given the power of choice, the possibility of making the wrong choice existed. Therefore, the plan of salvation was conceived in the mind of God before our first parents' rebellion in Eden.

In *The Desire of Ages*, we read this insightful statement: "The plan for our redemption was not an afterthought, a plan formulated after the fall of Adam. It was a revelation of 'the mystery which hath been kept in silence through times eternal.' Romans 16:25, R.V. It was an unfolding of the principles that from eternal ages have been the foundation of God's throne."[4]

The phrase "everlasting gospel" speaks of a God who loves the beings He created so much that, although He fully knew the consequences of their choices, He made provision for their eventual rebellion before it even happened.

There is another sense in which the gospel is eternal. To a generation starved for genuine, authentic love and longing for meaningful relationships, the gospel speaks of acceptance, forgiveness, belonging, grace, and life-changing power. It speaks of a God of unconditional love, who cares so deeply that He will go to any length to redeem us because He wants us with Him forever.

The eternal gospel speaks not only of the past and present but promises a future with hope. It speaks of living eternally with the One whose heart is aching to be with us forever. The gospel speaks of an eternal relationship with the Christ who created us and redeemed us so that we could live with Him through the ceaseless ages of eternity.

Considering the controversy between good and evil raging in the universe and Satan's distortion of God's character, the gospel of God's grace and boundless love will be preached to the ends of the earth as a witness of His eternal goodness.

What is the gospel? As shown to a dying thief at Calvary, it is the good news that salvation is a gift of God. He saves us not because we are good but because He is good. Our salvation is not dependent upon our works, but it is dependent on His grace. All our good works are motivated by love and empowered by grace. When Ellen White was asked whether the message of righteousness by faith detracted from the three angels' messages, her response was: "Several have written to me, inquiring if the message of justification by faith is the third angel's message, and I have answered, 'It is the third angel's message in verity.' "[5]

Righteousness by faith, God's unending love, and His abounding grace are not preambles to the three angels' messages. They are not a side dish until we get to the "meat" of the message. They are at the very heart of the three angels' messages.

This is the message of the everlasting gospel that is to rapidly go to the ends of the earth to prepare the world for the coming of Jesus.

We can never be ready to share the gospel unless we have experienced the gospel. And once we have truly experienced the salvation that Christ so freely offers and the grace that He so graciously bestows, we cannot be silent. The apostle Paul succinctly states, "For the love of Christ compels us" (2 Corinthians 5:14).

---

1. Ellen G. White, *Evangelism* (Washington, DC: Review and Herald®, 1946), 119, 120.

2. Portions of this chapter have been adapted from Mark Finley, "Radical Grace," *Adventist Review*, September 11, 2014, https://adventistreview.org/issue-archives/page -2014/page-9141526/141526-18/.

3. Ellen G. White, *The Desire of Ages* (Nampa, ID: CA: Pacific Press®, 2002), 753.

4. White, 22.

5. Ellen G. White, "Repentance the Gift of God," *Advent Review and Sabbath Herald*, April 1, 1890, 193.

4

"Fear God and Give Glory to Him"

The purpose of the book of Revelation is to prepare a people to be ready for Jesus' soon return—a people who will unite with Him in giving His last-day message to the world. The aged apostle John, exiled on Patmos, continues his urgent end-time appeal in Revelation 14 with these words: "Fear God and give glory to Him, for the hour of His judgment has come; and worship Him who made heaven and earth, the sea and springs of water" (verse 7).

Since the time in which we are now living is the final period of this earth's history, the everlasting gospel of Christ's redeeming grace leads us to make a total commitment of our lives to the One who gave His all for us. Let us meditate for a few moments on the expression "fear God and give glory to Him."

What does it mean to fear God?
The Greek New Testament word for "fear" in Revelation 14:7 is *phobeō*. It is used here not merely in the sense of being afraid of God but in the sense of reverence, awe, and respect. It conveys the

idea of absolute loyalty to God and full surrender to His will. It is an attitude of the mind that centers on God rather than self. Recognizing the immense love of God—His undying love revealed in the everlasting gospel on the cross of Calvary—we willingly respond in loving obedience.

Note this insightful statement in *The Desire of Ages*: "The exercise of force is contrary to the principles of God's government; He desires only the service of love; and love cannot be commanded; it cannot be won by force or authority. Only by love is love awakened. To know God is to love Him; His character must be manifested in contrast to the character of Satan."[1] God's character of love is the opposite of Lucifer's attitude, as shown in Isaiah 14:13, 14, when Lucifer says in his heart,

"I will ascend into heaven,
I will exalt my throne above the stars of God;
I will also sit on the mount of the congregation
On the farthest sides of the north;
I will ascend above the heights of the clouds,
I will be like the Most High."

The essence of the great controversy is submission to God. Lucifer was self-centered. He refused to submit to any authority except his own. Rather than submit to the One upon the throne, Lucifer desired to rule from the throne.

We discover the depth of the meaning of the expression "fear God" by observing its usage in other parts of the Bible. In Scripture, the fear—or reverence—of God leads to loving obedience of His commands.

Let us consider three passages that make this point crystal clear. Speaking to the Israelites, God instructs them to "fear the LORD your God, to keep all His statutes and His commandments which I command you" (Deuteronomy 6:2). In one of his psalms, David adds:

> Your hands have made me and fashioned me;
> Give me understanding, that I may learn Your commandments.
> Those who fear You will be glad when they see me,
> Because I have hoped in your word (Psalm 119:73, 74).

Ecclesiastes puts it too plainly to be misunderstood:

> Let us hear the conclusion of the whole matter:
>
> > Fear God and keep His commandments,
> > For this is man's all.
> > For God will bring every work into judgment,
> > Including every secret thing,
> > Whether good or evil (Ecclesiastes 12:13, 14).

In light of the judgment hour, Heaven's urgent appeal is for those saved by grace to live godly lives. Grace does not free us from obeying the commands of God. When we come in humble repentance, confessing our sins, His grace pardons us when we fail. That is why the apostle Paul states so emphatically in Romans 8:1: "There is therefore now no condemnation to those who are in Christ Jesus."

The gospel not only delivers us from the guilt of our past but also empowers us to live godly, obedient lives in the present. The apostle Paul declares that, as believers, "we have received grace and apostleship for obedience to the faith among all nations" (Romans 1:5).

There are some people who have the strange idea that salvation by grace somehow negates the law of God. They believe that any talk about obedience is legalism. They have declared, "All I want is Jesus." The question is, Which Jesus? A Jesus of our own making, or the Jesus of Scripture? The Christ of Scripture never leads us to downplay His law, which is the transcript of His character. The Christ of Scripture never leads us to minimize the doctrines of the Bible, which reveal more clearly who He is and what His plan is for this world. The Christ of Scripture never leads us to reduce His teaching to pious platitudes that are nonessential. Ellen White sets the record straight with this thought-provoking statement: "Those who are truly converted to Christ [must] keep on constant guard lest they accept error in place of truth. Those who think that it matters not what they believe in doctrine, so long as they believe in Jesus Christ, are on dangerous ground."[2] This is a striking statement. It clarifies the issue. You cannot separate Jesus from doctrine.

Christ is the embodiment of all doctrinal truth. Jesus is truth incarnated. He is doctrine lived out. Revelation's final appeal calls us through faith in Jesus to accept the fullness of everything He offers. It calls us to fear God and, by faith in His redeeming power, to live godly, obedient lives. As the religious philosopher Thomas à Kempis said, "Instant obedience is the only kind of obedience there is; delayed obedience is disobedience. Whoever strives to withdraw from obedience, withdraws from grace."

This is a remarkable statement and one that is totally aligned with the Bible's teaching. Grace always leads us to obey the commands of God. The issue is really one of allegiance and authority. Andrew Bonar, a noted Scottish theologian, puts it succinctly:

It is not the importance of the thing, but the majesty of the lawgiver, that is to be the standard of our obedience. . . .

Some, indeed, might reckon such minute and arbitrary rules as these as trifling. But the principle involved in obedience or

39

disobedience was none other than the same principle which was tried in Eden at the foot of the forbidden tree. It was really this—Is the Lord to be obeyed in *all* things whatsoever he commands? Is he a holy lawgiver? Are his creatures bound to give implicit assent to his will?[3]

The first angel's message is an urgent appeal, in light of heaven's judgment hour, to make God the center of our lives. In an age of materialism and consumerism, when secular values have made self the center, Heaven's appeal is to turn from the tyranny of self-centeredness and the bondage of self-inflated importance to place God at the center of our lives. For some, money is the center of their lives; for others, it is pleasure or power; and for still others, it is sports, music, or entertainment. Revelation's message is a clarion call to fear, respect, and honor God as life's true center.

In His masterful Sermon on the Mount, Jesus noted that we should not worry about what we will eat, drink, or wear. He then declares, "But seek first the kingdom of God and His righteousness, and all these things shall be added to you" (Matthew 6:33). Jesus asks, What are your priorities? Who has your allegiance? Where is your heart? Paul echoes this earnest appeal with these words: "Set your mind on things above, not on things on the earth" (Colossians 3:2).

The final battle in the great controversy between good and evil is for our minds. Our actions reveal what our thinking processes are. To fear God is to make Him first in our lives.

What does it mean to give glory to God?

Notice this contrast: fearing God speaks of an attitude of God-centered obedience. Giving glory to God speaks of our actions or how we live. Fearing God has to do with what we think. Giving glory to God has to do with what we do. Fearing God deals with our inner commitment to make God the center of our lives. Giving glory to God deals with how our inner convictions translate into a lifestyle that honors God in everything we do.

A lot of people have the idea that the treatment of their bodies is unrelated to their faith. They believe that their bodies are theirs to do with as they please. The apostle Paul implores, "I beseech [urge] you therefore, brethren, by the mercies of God, that you present your bodies a living sacrifice, holy, acceptable to God, which is your reasonable service" (Romans 12:1).

The New Testament Greek word for "bodies" is *sōmata*, which is better translated as the collective sum of who you are: body, mind, and emotions. The Phillips translation of the Bible renders "reasonable service" as "an act of intelligent worship." In other words, when you make a total commitment to "fear God" and "give glory to Him" in all you do, giving your mind, body, and emotions to Him, you are performing an act of intelligent worship.

According to the apostle Paul, our bodies are sanctuaries—the dwelling place of the Spirit of God—temples made holy by the presence of God. And he is emphatic: "If anyone defiles the temple of God, God will destroy him. For the temple of God is holy, which temple you are" (1 Corinthians 3:17).

Scripture gives us a clarion call to glorify God in every aspect of our lives. At a time when multitudes are abusing their bodies and damaging their brains with drugs, alcohol, and other destructive habits, God says, "I am calling you back to a life of faithful obedience. Place your body on the altar as a living sacrifice. Open your heart and mind to My Spirit so I can live in you. Then your body will truly be My temple."

When God is the center of our lives, our one desire is to give glory to Him in every aspect of our lives, whether our diet and the things we eat, our dress and the things we wear, our entertainment and the things we view, or our music and the things we listen to. We give glory to God as we reveal His character of love to the world through lives committed to doing His will. This is even more important in light of Earth's end-time judgment.

Any life focused primarily on self, narrowed down in the claustrophobic confines of its own littleness, is a very small life. The apostle Paul calls us to the largeness, the sublime greatness, of a life committed to service and dedicated to blessing others. He calls us to look beyond our own hurts, grief, and pain to touch someone else with God's grace. He calls us out of the pettiness of our small, self-made worlds to the largeness of the world Christ came to redeem. Just as the drink offering was poured out as a sacrifice on the ground in the Old Testament sanctuary service, so Paul's life was poured out as a sacrifice in the service of Christ.

There are some things in life that we may want to do that are not harmful in themselves, but we choose not to do them so that we will have more time to advance the cause of God. There are some pleasures we will not pursue for Christ's sake. There are some places we could go but will not visit because of our commitment to Christ's service. There are some things we could purchase, but we sacrificially choose not to buy them in order to advance the cause of Christ.

When you pour your life out for Christ's sake, it is not being wasted; it is being invested. We all pour out our lives for something. Some people pour out their lives in their work. Some people pour out their lives in sports. Some people pour out their lives in pleasure and entertainment. Some people pour out their lives in time-consuming, all-absorbing, mind-numbing digital devices.

Time is fleeting. We are living in Revelation's judgment hour. We are all pouring out our lives for something. One day fades into the next. One week quickly passes into the next month and the next year, and soon, the decades pass. The apostle Paul poured his life out for

Christ and the advancement of His kingdom. Are you pouring your life out for something that counts?

Revelation's overcomers

Revelation's message is one of victory, not defeat. It speaks of a people who, through God's grace and by His power, overcome. The word *overcome* is used eleven times, in one form or another, in Revelation. In the vision of the seven churches, representing the Christian church from the first century to our time, John says there are believers in every generation who will overcome. In the end time, those who overcome "shall inherit all things" (Revelation 21:7). This is not legalism. It is victory through Jesus Christ. It is faith in action. It is transforming, life-changing, and miraculous grace in the life of the believer.

Jesus' last-day message is an urgent appeal to live godly lives. It is a clarion call to holiness. One day God will have a group of people of whom it is written: "Here are those who keep the commandments of God and the faith of Jesus" (Revelation 14:12).

The only way anyone can keep the commandments of God is through the faith of Jesus. Notice that our text does not say "faith *in* Jesus," although that is extremely important. Rather, it says they have the "faith *of* Jesus," which is something more. It is the quality of faith that enabled Christ to be victorious over Satan's fiercest temptations.

Faith is a gift given to each believer. When we exercise faith, the Holy Spirit puts in our hearts faith that grows. We overcome, not by our willpower but by the power of the living Christ working through us. We overcome, not because of who we are but because of who He is.

We can overcome because He overcame. We can be victorious because He was victorious. We can triumph over temptation because He triumphed over temptation. Hebrews 4:14–16 states this powerfully: "Seeing then that we have a great High Priest who has passed through the heavens, Jesus the Son of God, let us hold fast our confession. For we do not have a High Priest who cannot sympathize with our weaknesses, but was in all points tempted as we are, yet without sin. Let us therefore come boldly to the throne of grace, that we may obtain mercy and find grace to help in time of need."

Jesus, the divine Son of God, has overcome the wiles of the devil. He faced temptation, trusting in the promises of God, surrendering His will to the Father's will, and depending on the Father's power. Trusting Him, looking to Him, believing in Him, we, too, can be victorious. Jesus is our all in all, and the three angels' messages are all about Him.

---

1. Ellen G. White, *The Desire of Ages* (Nampa, ID: Pacific Press®, 2002), 22.

2. Ellen G. White, *Christ Triumphant* (Hagerstown, MD: Review and Herald®, 1999), 235.

3. Andrew Bonar, *A Commentary on the Book of Leviticus*, 3rd ed. (London: James Nisbet, 1852), 211, 212; emphasis in the original.

5

The Good News
of the Judgment

The Bible's last book, Revelation, focuses on the end of the agelong controversy between good and evil. Lucifer, a rebel angel, challenged God's justice, fairness, and wisdom. He claimed that God is unfair and unjust in administering the universe. Revelation's final judgment is at the very center of this conflict over the character of God.

In previous chapters, we saw that God has sent a last-day message to humanity, pictured as three angels symbolically flying in midheaven to carry His final message to the ends of the earth. The foundation of this message is "the everlasting gospel" (Revelation 14:6). It is the good news of God's grace that changes us, transforms us, and delivers us from the condemnation and bondage of sin. When we are changed by grace and rejoice in the salvation that Christ so freely provides, we are motivated to cooperate with Him in sharing the message of His everlasting love.

Notice in Revelation 14:6, 7 that God's good news of "the everlasting gospel" includes the expression "the hour of His judgment is come." The hour of *whose* judgment has come? The text is clear. It is the hour of *God's* judgment. This is the hour for the entire universe to see the goodness of our God. Once and for all, the beings on unfallen worlds will see, in the light of the judgment hour, that God has done everything He could to save every human being. Christ's life and death revealed His character of unselfish love. The judgment reveals to the entire universe how Christ's infinite love pursued each person on Earth. It reveals His gracious actions to save every person who would respond in faith. It shows that the gospel has the power to change human lives.

Here are four facts about Revelation's end-time judgment that we need to remember.

1. The judgment reveals God's justice and mercy. In the universe's great controversy between good and evil, God finally answers Satan's charges that He is unfair and unjust in the final judgment. On the cross, Christ revealed His love before the entire universe. There is a price to be paid for sin, and Jesus Himself paid it. As a hymn writer puts it, "Jesus paid it all, / All to Him I owe."[1] In the judgment, He reveals His justice and His love in dealing with the sin problem.

When our names appear in judgment before God, Jesus will ask in the presence of the entire universe, "Could I have done anything more to save this individual?" Heaven's infinite, detailed records will be opened. We are so precious to God that the entire universe pauses to consider our choices in light of the wooing of the Holy Spirit and the redemption so freely provided by Christ on Calvary's cross.

The entire universe and the unfallen worlds will see the countless times God sent His Holy Spirit to our hearts. They will see how He sent angels to beat back the forces of Satan. They will see how He arranged the providences in our lives. They will see how He revealed Himself in the natural world. And they will see how He gave us opportunity after opportunity to respond to His loving appeals.

All of this was for one purpose: to save us. In the final analysis, every being in the universe will see that Calvary is enough—the Cross is sufficient. Jesus could do nothing more.

Revelation's judgment reveals God's unfathomable love and His justice in dealing with the controversy between good and evil. It shows once and for all, now and forever, in the present and throughout all eternity, that Heaven could have done nothing more to save us.

The judgment and the Cross are the intersection of justice and mercy. The broken law demands the death of the sinner. Justice declares, "The wages of sin is death," but mercy responds, "But the gift of God is eternal life in Christ Jesus our Lord" (Romans 6:23). If God's law could be changed or abolished, it would not have been necessary for Jesus to die. Christ's death establishes the eternal nature of the law, and the law is the basis for judgment. Revelation 20:12 makes this eternal truth plain: "And the dead were judged according to their works, by the things which were written in the books." Our works reveal our choices. Our deeds reveal our loyalty. Our good works, empowered by the Holy Spirit, do not save us, but they do testify that our faith is genuine. God's final judgment strips away all pretense, all hypocrisy, and all falsehood and pierces into the depths of our being. Christ reveals that He has done everything possible to save us, and the judgment reveals how we have responded to Christ's saving grace.

There is a second eternal truth in the three angels' announcements about the judgment that we cannot miss.

2. The judgment has arrived. It is a present-tense judgment. The hour of God's judgment is here. In Revelation 14:7, the angel declares in no uncertain terms that "the hour of His judgment has come." Here is an urgent, present-truth message for the entire world. Notice that our text does not say that "the hour of God's judgment *will* come." Instead, it emphatically announces that "the hour of His judgment *has* come," which is in the present tense.

This is only logical. According to Matthew 16:27, "the Son of Man will come in the glory of His Father with His angels, and then He will reward each according to his works."

Exiled on the island of Patmos, the apostle John, writing in the last chapter of the book of Revelation, highlights this announcement from Jesus, "And behold, I am coming quickly, and My reward is with Me, to give to every one according to his work" (Revelation 22:12).

Follow closely now. If Christ is coming to give out rewards, there must be a judgment before He comes to determine the rewards each person receives. This leads to these logical questions: Could we be living in the judgment hour now? Is time running out? Are we on the knife-edge of eternity? If the hour of God's judgment has come, when did this judgment begin?

We can find answers in the prophetic book of Daniel, which is a companion volume to the book of Revelation, pointing us to the unfolding events in the last days of Earth's history. The book of Revelation announces that the hour of God's judgment has come. The book of Daniel reveals when this judgment began. (In this chapter, we introduce the connection between Daniel's and Revelation's prophecies on the judgment. In the next chapter, we will study the exact timing of the beginning of the judgment.)

In Daniel 7, after describing Babylon, Media-Persia, Greece, Rome, the breakup of the Roman Empire, and the union of church and state throughout the centuries, God focuses Daniel's attention on a glorious celestial event that will set all things right. This is what Daniel sees in vision:

> "I watched till thrones were put in place,
> And the Ancient of Days was seated;
> His garment was white as snow,
> And the hair of His head was like pure wool.
> His throne was a fiery flame,

Its wheels a burning fire;
A fiery stream issued
And came forth from before Him.
A thousand thousands ministered to Him;
Ten thousand times ten thousand stood before Him.
The court was seated,
And the books were opened" (Daniel 7:9, 10).

The destiny of all humanity is decided in heaven's courtroom. The oppressive powers that persecute God's people are judged. Right prevails. Truth triumphs. Justice reigns. But this heavenly scene continues in Daniel 7:13:

"I was watching in the night visions,
And behold, One like the Son of Man,
Coming with the clouds of heaven!
He came to the Ancient of Days,
And they brought Him near before Him."

This is one of Scripture's most amazing, marvelous, and spectacular scenes. Jesus approaches His heavenly Father in the presence of the entire universe. Heavenly beings crowd around the throne of God. The entire universe of unfallen beings stands in awe of this judgment scene. The long conflict that has waged for millennia will soon be over. The battle for the throne of the universe will be fully, completely decided. Daniel states in verse 14:

"Then to Him was given dominion and glory and a kingdom,
That all peoples, nations, and languages should serve Him.
His dominion is an everlasting dominion,
Which shall not pass away,

49

And His kingdom the one
Which shall not be destroyed."

Jesus is worthy to receive the kingdom. Love has conquered. Grace is greater than sin—right triumphs over wrong.

3. *The judgment reveals the saving righteousness of Jesus and His triumph over the principalities and powers of hell.* "After these things I looked, and behold, a door standing open in heaven. And the first voice which I heard was like a trumpet speaking with me, saying, 'Come up here, and I will show you things which must take place after this' " (Revelation 4:1).

Jesus invites us to look through the open door in heaven's sanctuary to view eternal scenes in the great controversy between good and evil. He gives us a glimpse of the eternal plan of salvation as it plays out in heaven.

What do we see when we look through heaven's open door? What do we hear as we turn our ears heavenward? What issues are being decided in heaven's celestial court? We notice in Revelation 4:4 that twenty-four elders surround God's throne. Who are these twenty-four elders? In ancient Israel, there were twenty-four courses in the Levitical priesthood. These priests represented the people before God. In 1 Peter 2:9, the apostle declares that New Testament believers are a "chosen generation, a royal priesthood." These twenty-four elders represent all the redeemed who will rejoice around the throne of God one day. They are people of past ages who were resurrected at the time of Christ's resurrection and ascended to heaven with Him (Matthew 27:52).

This is good news. There are some of the redeemed from the earth around the throne of God. In every generation, there have been those who, by God's grace, have overcome through the power of the Holy Spirit.

The Good News of the Judgment

Who are the four living creatures in Revelation 4:6, 7? Remember, Jewish tradition tells us that Israel marched in the wilderness under four banners—a lion, a calf, the face of a man, and a flying eagle. These banners indicated God's continual protection and everlasting guidance and illustrated the roles Jesus would play in our rescue.

Jesus, the Lion of the tribe of Judah, left the glories of heaven and, in becoming a man, accepted the role of a sacrificial animal—the calf—but was resurrected and ascended to His Father's throne, flying through the heavens like a soaring eagle. These four living creatures praise Jesus through all eternity for His sacrificial love.

We see a throne set in heaven with God sitting upon it. There are divine beings around the throne. Soon all of heaven begins to sing, and the crescendo of praise swells higher and still higher:

"You are worthy, O Lord,
To receive glory and honor and power;
For You created all things,
And by Your will they exist and were created" (Revelation 4:11).

All of heaven praises Jesus, our all-powerful Creator, but in Revelation 5, the scene dramatically changes. Initially, the scene is no longer one of praise. Notice in Revelation 5:1 that there is the throne once again, and a scroll is introduced, written on both sides. It is sealed with divine seals, and no one in heaven or Earth can open the scroll.

In verse 2, the question is raised, "Who is worthy to open the scroll?" Heavenly beings tremble. The issue is serious. All humanity will be lost if no one in heaven can open the judgment scroll. No angelic being can represent humanity in Earth's final judgment. The apostle John, viewing the scene, recognizes its terrible significance.

In Revelation 5:3, John states, "And no one in heaven or on the earth or under the earth was able to open the scroll, or to look at it."

But wait! There is One who can open the scroll. There is One who is worthy to redeem humanity. There is One who bore the condemnation, the shame, the guilt, and the curse of sin.

John beholds the ultimate answer to the sin problem in Revelation 5:5, 6. Here, the aged prophet is shown the only way anyone can pass the final judgment at the throne of God. "But one of the elders said to me, 'Do not weep. Behold, the Lion of the tribe of Judah, the Root of David, has prevailed to open the scroll and to loose its seven seals' " (verses 5).

Jesus, the Lamb of God, who has sacrificed His life for the salvation of all humanity, takes the scroll of judgment and opens it. All of heaven bursts forth in rapturous praise. His victory over Satan's temptations, His death on Calvary's cross, His resurrection, and His high-priestly ministry provide salvation for all who choose to respond to His grace by faith.

Justice demands that the penalty for the broken law must be paid. Scripture is plain. Romans 3:23 states that "all have sinned and fall short of the glory of God." Romans 6:23 adds that "the wages of sin is death, but the gift of God is eternal life in Christ Jesus our Lord."

It is impossible for us to save ourselves. There is no way we can pass the judgment on our own. In light of the judgment bar of God, the debt we owe is much too high to pay.

4. The judgment is excellent news for the people of God. It signals the end of sin's reign and the deliverance of God's people. The judgment scene in Daniel 7, introduced earlier, is complementary to the judgment scenes in Revelation 5 and 14. In Daniel 7, Babylon, Media-Persia, Greece, and Rome rise and fall. The little horn arises out of Rome as a religiopolitical power that counterfeits the truth of God and persecutes the people of God.

Daniel's attention is then drawn from Earth to heaven, where God sits in judgment. As we read previously in Daniel 7:9, 10, all of heaven waits eagerly for the final verdict in heaven's judgment.

The Good News of the Judgment

Heavenly beings burst into rapturous song and rejoice as the kingdom is given to Jesus. But then, a marvel of all marvels, wonder of all wonders, see what happens next. We read about it in Daniel 7:22, 27:

"The Ancient of Days came, and a judgment was made in favor of the saints. . . .

" 'Then the kingdom and dominion,
And the greatness of the kingdoms under the whole heaven,
Shall be given to the people, the saints of the Most High.
His kingdom is an everlasting kingdom,
And all dominions shall serve and obey Him.' "

Jesus receives the kingdom and gives it to His faithful followers. In highest praise, we fall at His feet and worship Him through the ceaseless ages of eternity. Can anything be more encouraging? Jesus stands for us in the judgment. His perfect, righteous life covers our imperfections. His righteousness works within us to make us new. His grace pardons us, transforms us, and empowers us to live godly lives.

Fear is gone, and hell is defeated. Throughout the ceaseless ages of eternity, we will sing the praises and glory of Jesus. He redeemed us. He shed His blood for us. He sacrificed His life for us. He is our Savior, Redeemer, slain Lamb, interceding High Priest, living Christ, and coming King. Christ is all we need and everything our heart desires.

---

1. Elvina M. Hall, "Jesus Paid It All" (1865).

6

The Hour of His Judgment

In Daniel 8 and 9, we discover the divine timetable for the beginning of the heavenly judgment. Miraculously, in His infinite wisdom, God links this end-time judgment with specific milestones in the life of Jesus. These verifiable earthly events on the time line of history confirm the reliability of prophecy and the date for the beginning of the judgment. Daniel 8:14 gives us our first clue. The angel says to Daniel: "For two thousand three hundred days; then the sanctuary shall be cleansed."

Each Jew clearly understood the cleansing of the earthly sanctuary. It occurred at the end of the Jewish year and was a day of judgment. Although Daniel understood the concept of the cleansing of the sanctuary and the judgment, he was confused about the 2,300 days. At the end of chapter 8, we find him exclaiming, "I was astonished by the vision, but no one understood it" (verse 27).

You will recall that we previously discussed that one prophetic day equals one literal year. In Bible prophecy, when we have symbolic images, we also have symbolic time prophecies.

The next chapter, Daniel 9, records Daniel's earnest prayer to understand the vision. As he prays, the angel Gabriel comes in answer to his prayer. In Daniel 9:21, 22, we read, "While I was speaking in prayer, the man Gabriel, whom I had seen in the vision at the beginning, being caused to fly swiftly, reached me about the time of the evening offering. And he informed me, and talked with me, and said, 'O Daniel, I have now come forth to give you skill to understand.' "

Gabriel amazes Daniel as he reveals an answer to his prayer that is much broader than he could ever imagine. The angel Gabriel takes Daniel down the stream of time and reveals the truth about the coming Messiah, giving the exact dates of the beginning of His ministry and His cruel death. He then takes him centuries into the future and reveals the opening of God's judgment in heaven. This amazing prophecy chronicles the minute details of the future that only God could know.

The angel Gabriel then declares, "Understand, son of man, that the vision refers to the time of the end" (Daniel 8:17). What vision is Gabriel talking about? There is no vision given to Daniel in chapter 9. At the end of chapter 8, Daniel faints after Gabriel explains the portion of the vision related to time; therefore, Gabriel's explanation in chapter 9 must be regarding the portion of the prophecy Daniel did not understand in chapter 8. The vision of the 2,300 days in Daniel 8 and the cleansing of the sanctuary (verse 14), according to the angel Gabriel, applies to the time of the end (verse 17).

Some believe that the 2,300 days are literal days. They believe this little horn of Daniel 8 applies to the Seleucid leader Antiochus Epiphanes, who attacked Jerusalem and defiled the Jewish temple. But what does the Bible teach? God's Word makes it plain. Gabriel says that "the vision refers to the time of the end" (verse 17), and Antiochus certainly did not live at the time of the end.

The wording of Daniel 8 is fascinating. The ram—Media-Persia—is described as "great" (verse 4). The designation given to Cyrus, the Persian leader, is Cyrus the Great. The designation given to the male goat—Greece—is "very great" (verse 8). The designation given to Alexander is Alexander the Great. The little horn power that rises next is called "exceeding great" (verse 9). Whatever this new power is, it must be greater than Cyrus and Alexander. Antiochus Epiphanes was a little-known Seleucid leader, and he does not fit the specifications of this prophecy. I would rather accept what Gabriel says than any human opinion.

In Daniel 8, Gabriel begins his explanation of the 2,300-day prophecy. He describes the ram as representing Media-Persia and the male goat as representing Greece (verses 20, 21). He goes on to describe the little horn—pagan Rome. He then describes a religio-political power arising out of Rome that will establish an earthly priesthood and change God's law. But as he prepares to explain the time of the cleansing of the sanctuary, something happens to Daniel. He is overwhelmed and confused by what Gabriel has shown him—so much so that he faints. At the end of chapter 8, we see that Daniel does not understand this vision and needs divine guidance.

The vision explained
Gabriel reappears and reassures the aged prophet. "Daniel, I have now come forth to give you skill to understand" (Daniel 9:22). He continues in verse 23: "At the beginning of your supplications the command went out, and I have come to tell you, for you are greatly beloved; therefore consider the matter, and understand the vision."

What encouragement this must have brought to Daniel! Gabriel calls Daniel "greatly beloved." As for the vision, Gabriel continues, "Therefore consider the matter, and understand the vision." What matter—and what vision? The matter that Gabriel was discussing in chapter 8—when Daniel fainted and did not understand—was the cleansing of the sanctuary. The vision is of the 2,300 days. As we have noted, since there is no vision recorded in chapter 9, Gabriel must be speaking of the portion of the vision in Daniel 8 that the prophet did not understand. Gabriel continues:

"Seventy weeks are determined
For your people and for your holy city,
To finish the transgression,
To make an end of sins,
To make reconciliation for iniquity,
To bring in everlasting righteousness,
To seal up vision and prophecy,
And to anoint the Most Holy" (Daniel 9:24).

A divine timetable

Gabriel continues explaining this remarkable timetable of prophecy in verse 25:

"Know therefore and understand,
That from the going forth of the command
To restore and build Jerusalem
Until Messiah the Prince,
There shall be seven weeks and sixty-two weeks."

With divine insight, the prophecy reveals specific dates on the Messianic time line. As mentioned in chapter 1, in Bible prophecy, one prophetic day equals one literal year (Ezekiel 4:6; Numbers 14:34). Please do not misunderstand. When a day is spoken of in the Bible, it is generally a literal day. For example, the book of Genesis says, "The evening and the morning were the first day" (Genesis 1:5). That is a day—a twenty-four-hour period.

57

But when we study the symbols of prophecy, things are not always as they seem. Have you ever walked down the street and seen a lion with an eagle's wings or a leopard with four heads and wings? When it is obvious that the images are symbolic, then the time periods are symbolic. In Daniel and Revelation, where there are symbolic time periods and symbolic imagery, then the time periods are symbolic. In the prophecies of Daniel and Revelation, the day-year principle especially applies.

Seventy weeks are composed of 490 days. Since one prophetic day equals one literal year, 490 prophetic days are 490 literal years. Seventy weeks, or 490 days (years), apply specifically to the Jewish nation and the coming of the Messiah. They are determined for Daniel's people—the Jews. What does the Hebrew word for "determined" mean? The Old Testament book of Daniel was written in Aramaic and Hebrew, and the interesting Hebrew word *chathak* (*khaw-thak*) has been translated as "determined." A literal translation of this word means "to cut off" or "to separate from."

Gabriel tells Daniel that 490 years are cut off, or separated from, the 2,300 years. These 490 years—the first portion of the 2,300 years—apply to the Jews. Gabriel continues his explanation by telling Daniel what would happen during that first 490-year period. This most thrilling prophecy shows that God does things on time.

Going on, Gabriel then explains to Daniel when this period begins. He states in verse 25:

> "Know therefore and understand,
> That from the going forth of the command
> To restore and build Jerusalem
> Until Messiah the Prince,
> There shall be seven weeks and sixty-two weeks;
> The street shall be built again, and the wall,
> Even in troublesome times."

Gabriel knows Daniel's concerns for his captive people, so he starts with an extremely important event to Daniel—the command to restore and rebuild Jerusalem. In other words, Daniel is told that when he hears the Persian decree for the Jews to return to their homeland, rebuild the crumbling walls of Jerusalem, and restore the temple worship services, the prophetic time line of his prophecy would begin. The angel's explanation is plain. The time period is specific. When the decree to rebuild the walls of Jerusalem is issued, and the Jews are allowed to return from captivity, there will be sixty-nine prophetic weeks until the coming of the Messiah.

How much time is sixty-nine prophetic weeks? Again, we saw from the books of Ezekiel and Numbers that one prophetic day equals a literal year. So, 69 weeks times the 7 days in each week amounts to 483 days—483 years. From the decree to restore and rebuild Jerusalem to the Messiah, Jesus Christ, would be exactly 483 years. When did this decree go forth to restore and rebuild Jerusalem?

We discover the answer in Ezra 7. Several decrees were issued by Medo-Persian kings, but it was the third one, issued by Artaxerxes, that allowed the Jews not only to return to their homeland but also to restore sanctuary worship with a priesthood, enabling them once again to establish themselves as a religious community. King Artaxerxes said, "I issue a decree that all those of the people of Israel and the priests and Levites in my realm, who volunteer to go up to Jerusalem, may go" (verse 13). This detailed decree continues for several verses until we find Ezra's response in verse 27: "Blessed be the LORD God of our fathers, who has put such a thing as this in the king's heart, to beautify the house of the LORD which is in Jerusalem."

According to Ezra, the decree to restore and rebuild Jerusalem was issued by Artaxerxes in the autumn of 457 BC. From this decree in 457 BC until the Messiah would be 69 weeks or 483 years.

Imagine that we are walking forward on a time line. If we start with the decree in 457 BC, and take one step for each year, proceeding 457 years forward, we would arrive at the year zero. But of course, there was never a year zero in history. The time line of history does not include the year zero. It goes from 1 BC to AD 1. So we take 457 steps, and when we get to 1 BC and take our last step, we do not get to year zero but to AD 1. We still have 26 years left of the 483 years. These additional 26 years take us from AD 1 to AD 27.

The Bible says "that from the going forth of the command / To restore and build Jerusalem / Until Messiah the Prince" (Daniel 9:25), there will be a span of 69 prophetic weeks—483 years. In other words, according to the Bible, the Messiah would appear in AD 27.

The word *Messiah* means "the anointed one." And do you know what happened precisely in AD 27? In that exact year, Jesus Christ, the Messiah, was baptized. The book of Daniel predicted the precise date of the baptism of Christ hundreds of years in advance. As Luke's Gospel teaches us, Jesus was baptized in the fifteenth year of Tiberius Caesar—AD 27 (Luke 3:1–3, 21). Jesus worked with Joseph in the carpenter shop of Nazareth until He was thirty years old. At the age of thirty, He was baptized. Then He began His role as the Messiah and commenced His ministry, which continued for three and a half years. The Bible prophecy in Daniel 9 predicted these events in the life of Christ hundreds of years in advance. Prophecy does not guess. It knows. Events in God's timetable happen as they have been predicted.

The Crucifixion predicted

There is much more to come in this remarkable prophecy. "And after the sixty-two weeks / Messiah shall be cut off, but not for Himself" (Daniel 9:26). Cut off? What does this mean? It means that He would be crucified. The verse adds, "But not for Himself." In other words, Christ's death on Calvary's cross was for us. He died for us. He died the death that was ours so we could live the life that was His. He died for sins in which He had no share so we could freely receive the gift of grace in His sinless life. The text also says this:

> "And the people of the prince who is to come
> Shall destroy the city and the sanctuary.
> The end of it shall be with a flood,
> And till the end of the war desolations are determined"
> (verse 26).

This refers to the destruction of the city of Jerusalem and the earthly sanctuary by Titus in AD 70.

Let us continue studying Gabriel's message from Daniel 9:27: "Then he"—that is, Jesus—"shall confirm a covenant with many for one week; / But in the middle of the week / He shall bring an end to sacrifice and offering."

Daniel is told that 70 weeks were determined for the Jews, and now he knew—and we now know—that by AD 27, 69 of those weeks, or 483 years, would be used up. There would be one week left. One prophetic week from AD 27—seven years beyond AD 27—takes us to AD 34. The Bible says that sometime in the middle of this week—in the midst of this last seven years—the Messiah would be crucified. The middle point of seven years, or half of seven, is three and a half. Gabriel tells Daniel that the Messiah would be crucified three and a half years from AD 27.

We know from Ezra that the decree to rebuild and restore Jerusalem went forth in the fall of 457 BC. And 483 years on, our time line takes us to the fall of AD 27, the exact year of Christ's baptism. Now, if we were to proceed an additional three and a half years from the fall of AD 27, where would that take us? Precisely to the spring of AD 31. In the middle of this seventieth week, in AD 31, Jesus was crucified, and the high priest tore his garments, sealing the Jewish leaders' rejection of the Messiah. And finally, in AD 34, Stephen, the first Christian martyr, was stoned (Acts 6:8–7:60), launching the gospel to the Gentiles.

The time of the end

Remember, this is just the first portion of the larger 2,300-year prophecy. You see, Gabriel not only explained to Daniel the 490 years that related to his people, the Jews, but also the rest of the 2,300 years, which apply to you and me. The first 490 years of the 2,300-year prophecy were designated for the Jewish nation. This first portion of the prophecy ran out in AD 34.

The last part of the 2,300 years has to do with God's people today, the cleansing of the heavenly sanctuary, and the second coming of Christ. Prophecy ties an event we can see, the first coming of Christ, with an event in the future, the second coming of Christ. And as the events of the first part of the prophecy came true with amazing accuracy, the predicted events of the second part of this prophecy obviously will come true.

Let us reread Daniel 8:14: "And he said to me, 'For two thousand three hundred days; then the sanctuary shall be cleansed.' " Since one prophetic day equals one literal year, the 2,300 years must take us down to the time of the end, just as the angel Gabriel revealed. We know that the first 490 years applied to the Jews and ended in AD 34. Subtracting 490 years from 2,300 years leaves us with 1,810 years. These 1,810 years apply to God's people at the end time. If we begin at AD 34 and proceed 1,810 years down the prophetic time line, we arrive at AD 1844. To explain it another way, if you start in the fall of 457 BC and go forward 2,300 years, you go to the fall of AD 1844.

We are living in the time of the cleansing of the heavenly sanctuary or the judgment hour. This is no common time. This is no ordinary time. The words of Daniel the prophet come echoing down the centuries: "For two thousand three hundred days; then the sanctuary shall be cleansed" (verse 14). Every Jew understood that the cleansing of the earthly sanctuary on the Day of Atonement meant a day of judgment. All those who did not repent of their sins were "cut off" from the camp of Israel. The Israelites were to afflict their souls in confession and repentance for their sins (Leviticus 23:29, 30). The cleansing of the sanctuary speaks of Earth's final judgment before the coming of Jesus, as described in Revelation 14:7.

In the light of heaven's end-time judgment, God makes His final appeal to all humans everywhere to respond to His love, accept His grace, and live godly, obedient lives. At the end of these 2,300 years of prophetic time, God's judgment hour begins.

Soon, the great controversy between good and evil will be finished. Soon, the wicked powers will be judged and found guilty. Then God's people will be declared righteous through the grace of Christ.

We are living in the judgment hour. Since 1844, God has been restoring the truth of Scripture to the world—truth that has been lost sight of down through the centuries and obscured by human tradition.

Time is running out. Is there anything in your life that is not in harmony with God's will—anything in your life that separates you from Him? Do you spend time in His Word? Do you long to know Him from His Word? Do you hunger for the truth in His Word? Are you willing to lay aside all human traditions and man-made doctrines to obey this Christ? Why not join me in saying yes to Him?

7

Worshiping the Creator

In the 1840s, social, political, scientific, and religious revolutions changed the world. In 1844, Charles Darwin published an essay espousing an early version of his theory of evolution. Also in 1844, Karl Marx began fleshing out communist ideals in his *Economic and Philosophic Manuscripts of 1844*—a precursor to *The Communist Manifesto*, which would eventually be published worldwide. That same year Samuel Morse first sent a telegraph message from Washington, DC, to Baltimore, Maryland.[1]

In 1859, Darwin's *On the Origin of Species* was published, setting forth a more developed version of evolutionary theory. One website, addressing the long-standing influence of that book, states that it "remains one of history's most influential and talked about scientific papers. It introduced the theory that populations evolve over the course of generations through a process of natural selection, a theory that became the backbone of modern biology."[2]

The impact of evolutionary thought on science, philosophy, psychology, and religion is incalculable. If we evolved—if we are products of fortuitous chance and nothing more than a collection of genes and chromosomes—life has little meaning. The essence of life becomes self-gratification. Personal happiness becomes life's reckless pursuit. Life has lost its true meaning if human beings are merely enlarged protein molecules. If we are some aberration of nature, some random collection of chemical components, and some chance arrangement of cells, we become little more than advanced animals.

Extreme socialism, combined with Karl Marx's oft-quoted statement that religion "is the opium of the people,"[3] and the centralization of all power to a select few who considered workers, or the proletariat, as building blocks in the wall of the state further led to the dehumanization of human beings. These two movements—evolution and communism—developed simultaneously and placed an extremely low value on all human life by dismissing the concept of a personal God who is the Creator of the universe.

In the 1840s, God raised up a divine movement of destiny to proclaim His last-day message to a world longing to discover meaning, purpose, and identity. A group of Bible-believing Christians from multiple faith backgrounds began studying the age-old prophecies of Daniel and Revelation. There they discovered a message tailor-made for the times—a message suited to answer the great questions of a generation anticipating the soon return of Christ.

Leo Buscaglia, the popular motivational speaker, once declared, "It's not enough to have lived. We should be determined to live for something."[4] Russian author Fyodor Dostoevsky stated it well: "The mystery of human existence lies not in just staying alive, but in finding something to live for."[5] Revelation's message provides just such a purpose.

Worship the Creator

In the last few chapters, we have discovered that the expression "fear

God and give glory to Him" (Revelation 14:7) speaks of making God, not ourselves, the center of our lives. This inner commitment of absolute loyalty to God results in living lives of obedience to His will and pleasing Him in all we do. The decision to dedicate our lives entirely to God is made more urgent in the blazing light of eternity. In Revelation 14:7, the angel announces a present-tense judgment. He cries with a loud voice, "The hour of His [God's] judgment has come." We also discovered that we have been living in the judgment hour since 1844. It is no longer business as usual. Heaven's urgent appeal is to get ready for the coming of Jesus.

Revelation 14:7 ends with an appeal to "worship Him who made heaven and earth, the sea and springs of water." These words perfectly mirror those found in the Sabbath commandment in Exodus 20. They are a clarion call to worship the Creator at a time when most of the scientific and religious world has accepted the theory of Darwinian evolution. Revelation's final appeal is rooted in the Bible's first book—Genesis. We will never fully understand the issues in this cosmic battle over worship unless we understand the significance of creation.

Why creation matters
Let us return to the beginning of the Bible to understand better the end of the Bible. Genesis 1:1 declares, "In the beginning God created the heavens and the earth." This verse is the foundation for all of Scripture: "In the beginning God created." The Hebrew word for "create" in this passage is *bara'*. It refers to something God did. This Hebrew verb is linked to God's creative activity. God has the ability, the awesome power, to create something out of nothing. God speaks, and the earth comes into existence.

The prophet Isaiah beckons us to meditate on God's creative power with these words:

Worshiping the Creator

Lift up your eyes on high,
And see who has created these things,
Who brings out their host by number;
He calls them all by name,
By the greatness of His might
And the strength of His power;
Not one is missing (Isaiah 40:26).

Creation reveals a God of awesome might and unlimited power. His creative power not only brought the heavens and Earth into existence but has worked on behalf of His people through the centuries. God's creative power delivered Israel from Egyptian bondage and parted the Red Sea. The Red Sea is not a tiny puddle of water in the Middle East; it is a vast sea. Some Jewish scholars believe that the Israelites crossed the Red Sea at the point of the Gulf of Suez. The Gulf of Suez's maximum width is twenty miles, and its average depth is 131 feet. The power of God to part those waters to deliver His people was enormous.

His eternal power still parts the troubled waters of our lives. He still opens the way where there is no way. He is still the God who delivers us from the hand of the oppressor. For those who trust Him, His power is still exercised in remarkable ways.

God's creative power also formed the manna that fed Israel for forty years in the desert. It was His creative power that provided for the Israelites' needs in their wilderness wanderings. He is still the God of creation who provides, still the God who cares, and still the God whose creative power meets our needs.

It was God's creative power that covered the Israelites with the cloud by day to protect them from the scorching heat of the desert and provided the pillar of fire to warm them from the chill of the night. He is still the God of creation who guides our lives.

Throughout the centuries, He has been and still is the God of creation who has not forgotten His creation. He is the God of beginnings who is with us to the end of time. He is the God who began this world, is ever present in this world, and will never forsake His people of this world. He is the God who delivers, the God who provides, and the God who guides. The God of creation is the God of unlimited power. He is the God of the impossible.

Facing temptation
Every single one of us faces battles with temptation every day. The good news is that the same God who unleashed His infinite power to create the world unleashes that infinite power to defeat the forces of evil that wage the battle for our souls. Jesus has something more to offer than frustrating defeat. He has something more to offer than repeated failure. He has something more to offer than stumbling on the same point again and again. Who is it that we serve? He is the all-powerful Creator with unlimited, infinite power that is ours when we grasp it by faith. We are transformed, changed, and made new by the Creator's power.

There is an amazing truth in 2 Corinthians 5:17: "Therefore, if anyone is in Christ, he is a new creation; old things have passed away; behold, all things have become new." Let us make this truth very practical. This week ask God to help you more deeply and completely understand how His creative power can change your life. Here is a simple prayer: Dear Lord, You are the Creator of this world and everything in it. You are the God of awesome power. By faith, I believe You can make my life a new creation. I surrender to You anything out of harmony with Your will and ask You to re-create Your image in me.

Creation speaks of the infinite power available in the battle between good and evil in each of our lives. This is why creation matters. Creation speaks of an all-powerful God who can re-create our hearts in His image. Creation speaks of a God who, in the last days, gives us the strength to overcome Satan's fiercest temptations, his most cunning enticements, and his most subtle deceptions. Revelation's call to worship the Creator is a call to live praise-filled lives that rejoice in the strength that He gives us to face each day.

There is another aspect of worshiping the Creator that really matters: creation speaks of a God of intricate design and careful planning, who is the Originator of life. The book of beginnings, Genesis, tells us the story of Creation. The planets orbit the sun in an orderly, predictable pattern. The tides rise and fall in an orderly, predictable pattern. Fruit trees predictably produce fruit after their kind. Orange trees produce oranges, and apple trees produce apples.

Everywhere we turn in nature, we clearly see intelligent design. Whether it is these amazing human bodies of ours in their intricate complexity or the natural world around us in things as simple as the beauty of flowers, the flight of birds, or the majesty of a sunrise—all of nature indicates order and symmetry, not randomness and chance.

Creation speaks of a divine plan. Since God created us, we are valuable in His sight. Whatever the circumstances of our lives, we are special to God. If we allow Him to, He will work out His plan for our lives day by day. The One who created us will never forget us. Psalm 48 shares this amazing thought:

> For this is God,
> Our God forever and ever;
> He will be our guide
> Even to death (verse 14).

Did you catch the significance of this divine truth? Our Creator is ever present with us to guide our lives. He is the all-powerful, all-knowing, and ever-present God. The psalmist declares:

I will praise You, for I am fearfully and wonderfully made;
Marvelous are Your works,
And that my soul knows very well.
My frame was not hidden from You,
When I was made in secret,
And skillfully wrought in the lowest parts of the earth
How precious also are Your thoughts to me, O God!
How great is the sum of them!
If I should count them, they would be more in number than
    the sand;
When I awake, I am still with You
(Psalm 139:14, 15, 17, 18).

Did you grasp the significance of David's words? God thinks about us more times each day than there are grains of sand at the seaside. In other words, there is never a time when we are not in God's mind. God has a purpose for your life. The Creator has a divine plan even when things do not seem to go right. Have the following thoughts ever flooded into your mind? *I have committed my life to Christ. I am attempting to live for God and serve Him, so why are there so many obstacles? Why does the devil seem to attack my family and me? I just do not understand.*

Through the circumstances of life, our loving Creator is working out His divine plans, even if we do not recognize or understand them. He is worthy of our worship because He has given us life. He sustains our lives, and He works through all the circumstances of life, good or bad, to draw us closer to Him.

Creation is the basis for our worship
The very basis for all worship is that God created us. As the psalmist says, we are "fearfully and wonderfully made" (verse 14). In Revelation 4:11, John adds,

70

Worshiping the Creator

"You are worthy, O Lord,
To receive glory and honor and power;
For You created all things,
And by Your will they exist and were created."

Human beings exist but not through some process of evolutionary randomness. Before we were ever conceived in the womb of our mothers, we were conceived in the mind of God. Life is a precious gift given by God. True worship always acknowledges the "God who created all things through Jesus Christ" (Ephesians 3:9).

Our existence is not the result of blind chance or happenstance. It is the purposeful act of God. This is why the psalmist could state, "He fashions their hearts individually" (Psalm 33:15).

The Lord Himself speaks this almost incredible truth to the prophet Jeremiah: "Before I formed you in the womb I knew you; / Before you were born I sanctified you; / I ordained you a prophet to the nations" (Jeremiah 1:5).

In our search for meaning, we have only one of two options: either life is the result of pure biological chance, or life is a gift of God, with purpose and meaning.

Since we live in a world of brokenness and sin, we often experience less-than-ideal circumstances. In this world, there are physical and mental deformities. But all life is precious to God. Those who are less fortunate are not less valuable to God. Human beings are not defined by their intellectual capacities or their physical abilities. Human life has worth because a divine Creator brought us into existence and has a purpose for each individual.

Since life is the purposeful act of God, all life is sacred, whether that is the life of the unborn or the life of the aged. When we worship God as the Creator, we acknowledge the sanctity of life. Since every human being is unique, to lightly regard life is a sin against the

Creator of all life. The call to worship the Creator is the call to understand the value of every human being.

Creation speaks of our value in God's sight. It speaks of our worth to Him. We are not alone in the universe—some speck of cosmic dust. He created us. He fashioned us. And He made us. We did not evolve. We are not a genetic accident. Jesus is worthy of our worship because He not only created us but also redeemed us. Creation and Redemption are at the heart of all true worship.

---

1. Portions of this chapter were adapted from Mark A. Finley, "The Three Angels' Messages: Antiquated Message or Relevant Present Truth?" *Ministry*, August 2021, https://www.ministrymagazine.org/archive/2021/08/The-three-angels-messages.

2. "First Draft of Darwin's Origin of Species Goes Online," Science, CBC News, April 17, 2008, https://www.cbc.ca/news/science/first-draft-of-darwin-s-origin-of -species-goes-online-1.766695.

3. Karl Marx, *Critique of Hegel's "Philosophy of Right,"* trans. Annette Jolin and Joseph O'Malley, ed. Joseph O'Malley (New York: Cambridge University Press, 1970), 131.

4. Wikiquote, s.v. "Leo Buscaglia," last modified March 31, 2021, https://en.wiki quote.org/wiki/Leo_Buscaglia.

5. Fyodor Dostoevsky, *The Brothers Karamazov*, trans. Andrew R. MacAndrew (New York: Bantam Books, 1980), 306.

8

The Sabbath and the End

The casualties on both sides were high. The shelling was intense. Heavy bombardment from the artillery lasted all day. The ground shook violently from the constant pounding of German aircraft. The Allied forces responded with firefights of their own. Rival armies faced each other across the trenches.

Joe, an eighteen-year-old Allied soldier, leaned back against the earthen wall of his freshly dug trench, exhausted. The sun was setting. Another day had passed, and he was still alive. It was Christmas Eve 1914.

Thoughts of home flooded his mind: Mom, Dad, his brother, Tom, and his sister, Alice. Freshly baked apple pie, homemade raisin cookies, roast turkey, and mashed potatoes. Colorfully wrapped presents under the Christmas tree, smiles and hugs, and logs burning in the fireplace. Hot chocolate—peace.

But in this nightmare called war, death stared him in the face. "On earth peace, [and] goodwill toward men" were only figments of his imagination (Luke 2:14). The battlefield was quiet now. The air was crisp and clear. The stars twinkled in a moonlit sky. It was the eve of the famous Christmas truce.

Then he heard it. Could it be singing? Were his ears deceiving him this Christmas Eve? Was this a subtle trap? Was it some sinister plot? The sounds of a familiar Christmas carol gladdened the night air.

Although the words were being sung in German, the tune was unmistakable: "Silent night, holy night, / All is calm, all is bright; / Round yon virgin mother and Child . . ."[1]

German soldiers sang Christmas carols a few hundred yards away. Slowly, cautiously at first, Joe pulled himself out of his foxhole. His heart was touched. His emotions were stirred. Suddenly, he could not restrain himself any longer. Spontaneously, he began singing, "Silent night, holy night." His American colleagues joined in the singing: "Silent night, holy night, all is calm, all is bright."

Soon, voices that had shouted the curses of war a few hours before now echoed a chorus of praise. The two opposing sides approached each other. They embraced. They laughed. They sang. For one night, they were brothers. They shared a common humanity. The fighting stopped. The bombing ceased. The mortars were silent. On that Christmas Eve, for just a moment, enemies became friends.

They recognized a profound truth found in Acts 17:24, 26: "God, who made the world and everything in it, since He is Lord of heaven and earth, does not dwell in temples made with hands. . . . And He has made from one blood every nation of men to dwell on all the face of the earth, and has determined their preappointed times and the boundaries of their dwellings."

Evolution is dehumanizing

For one shining moment, the soldiers embraced their Creator and Savior, who had come to Earth. Only the God of creation provides a true sense of hope and self-worth. The Creator of the universe created us. Each of us is special. When your genes and chromosomes came together to form the unique biological structure of your personality, God threw away the pattern.

Evolution is dehumanizing. If I am an enlarged protein molecule, if I am simply the product of fortuitous chance, or if I am only an advanced form of animal, life has little meaning. I am merely one of eight billion people clawing at one another for living space on a planet called Earth.

By contrast, creation provides a moral imperative for living. God has created me, and I am accountable to Him for my actions. The One who made me and holds me responsible has established absolutes in a world of moral relativism.

The first angel of Revelation 14 declares that "the hour of His judgment has come" (verse 7). Since God created us with the capacity to make moral choices, we are responsible for the decisions we make. If we were merely a random collection of cells or products of our heredity and environment, our actions would be determined by forces over which we have no control. Judgment implies moral responsibility. In this crisis hour of Earth's history, the judgment hour, God calls us to make decisions in the light of eternity.

Evolution provides no moral ethic for living. Since it proclaims that humans are advanced animals, the highest standard is the human mind. Morality is determined from within. There is no absolute, eternal standard to govern behavior. Creation, by contrast, provides us with a sense of direction and purpose. The God who created us provides, in His Word, guidelines for living. His commands are always for our good. We are not left alone to battle with life's forces. He has revealed what is right in His Word and gives us the power to do what is right through His Holy Spirit.

Evolution looks within to find strength for life's trials. Creation looks without. It looks to a loving, powerful, and all-knowing God.

Creation provides a sense of destiny. The God who loves me, created me, and cares for me has prepared a place in heaven for me. Death is not a long night without a morning. The grave is not a dark hole in the ground. God has a glorious new tomorrow planned.

For the evolutionist, death is the end. There is no tomorrow. But creation speaks of a bright tomorrow. One day suffering will be over, and the God who created the world in the beginning will create "new heavens and a new earth" (2 Peter 3:13).

Evolution echoes uncertainty about the future. Creation speaks of a certain future. Evolution offers no hope of eternal life. Creation answers the eternal questions of life: Where did I come from? Why am I here? Where am I going? Evolution provides a distorted view of life's origin, fails to address the question of life's purpose, and leaves the soul barren regarding life's ultimate destiny.

Creation unites us with God. It establishes our self-worth. It forges ties with all humanity. It creates a common ancestry. It inspires confidence in a God who cares. It links us to God's inexhaustible power. And it encourages us with the hope of life after death.

Creation and the Sabbath

What do we call the One who made heaven, earth, and sea? The Creator. The Bible instructs us to worship the Creator. "The Revelation of Jesus Christ" is a call to worship Jesus as the Creator (Revelation 1:1). We understand this more clearly when we notice Ephesians 3:9: "Make all see what is the fellowship of the mystery, which from the beginning of the ages has been hidden in God who created all things through Jesus Christ."

Satan has attempted to distort the idea of creation because he hates Jesus and does not want Him to receive the worship due Him as our Creator and Redeemer. The Sabbath is at the center of the great controversy over Christ's worthiness to receive worship as our

Creator. God's last-day message calls all humanity back to worship Christ as the Creator of heaven and Earth. The basis for all worship is the fact that He created us. Accept evolution, and you destroy the very foundation for worship. John the revelator succinctly states this idea with these words:

"You are worthy, O Lord,
To receive glory and honor and power;
For You created all things,
And by Your will they exist and were created" (Revelation 4:11).

Christ is worthy precisely because He created all things. If God did not create us—if we merely evolved, and life is a cosmic accident based on chance and random selection—there is absolutely no reason to worship. In an age of evolution, the Sabbath is an eternal symbol of God's creative power and authority. The Sabbath is a weekly reminder that we are not our own. God created us. Life cannot exist apart from Him, "for in Him we live and move and have our being" (Acts 17:28).

A link to our family of origin

The Sabbath calls us back to our roots. It is a link to our family of origin. The Sabbath has been observed continuously since time began. It is an unbroken connection back through time to our Creator. The Sabbath tells us that we are not just a product of time plus chance. It keeps us focused on the glorious truth that we are the children of God. It calls us to an intimate, close relationship with Him.

When Schia was four years old, her baby brother was born. Little Schia began to ask her parents to leave her alone with the new baby. They were concerned about leaving a four-year-old with the new baby, so they said, "Schia, when you are a little older but not now." Over time, though, Schia was so loving toward the new little one that they changed their minds and decided to let her have her private conference with "Baby." Elated, Schia went into the baby's room and shut the door, but it opened a crack, enough for her curious parents to peek in and listen. They saw little Schia walk up quietly to her baby brother, put her face close to his, and say, "Baby, tell me what God feels like. I am starting to forget."

The truth is, we all tend to forget. The frantic pace of the week, the struggle to survive, and the hectic nature of twenty-first-century living combine, at times, to make us lose focus and forget the real purpose of life. That is why God says, "Remember." The Sabbath is a weekly reminder of what God is like. It calls us to a new relationship with Him.

A deception

The great controversy that began in heaven millennia ago was over the question of God's authority. Satan claimed that God was unfair and unjust. He rebelled against the eternal laws of the universe, given by a loving God to maintain heaven's peace and joy. In the Garden of Eden, Satan used the same tactics with Eve. He insinuated doubt and suggested that she did not have to obey God. He presented God's commands as arbitrary.

Eve and her husband, Adam, failed to discern God's love in His command and plunged the entire human race into the world of sin and death. Obedience to God's commands, flowing from a heart that trusts Him, is essential. The Sabbath is not some arbitrary command. It is at the very heart of worship. It is part of God's last-day message to the world. It is a perpetual reminder that He is the Creator, and we are His creatures.

Notice the significance of the Sabbath in Revelation 14:7, 9, 10, 12. Revelation 14:7 is a call to worship the Creator: "Fear God and give glory to Him, for the hour of His judgment has come; and worship Him who made heaven and earth, the sea and springs of water." Revelation 14:9, 10 is a solemn appeal not to worship the beast: "Then a third angel followed them, saying with a loud voice, 'If anyone worships the beast and his image, and receives his mark on his forehead or on his hand, he himself shall also drink of the wine of the wrath of God.'" Revelation 14:12 describes the people who worship the Creator and do not worship the beast: "Here is the patience of the saints; here are those who keep the commandments of God and the faith of Jesus." These passages make it clear that worship is the central issue in the conflict between good and evil—Christ and Satan—in the last days.

Two ways of worshiping are contrasted in these verses—worshiping the Creator and worshiping the beast. We have already discovered that the Sabbath is God's eternal sign of worshiping Him as the Creator. Revelation 14:12 reveals that those who have "the faith of Jesus" are loyal to God in Earth's final crisis and keep His commandments in the face of ridicule, opposition, persecution, and death. The heart of the Sabbath is a relationship acknowledging that God is worthy of our most supreme devotion, our deepest allegiance, and our total loyalty.

Revelation's end-time message of worshiping the Creator is a message of the One who re-creates. He can give us victory over those health-destroying habits, those un-Christlike attitudes, and those addictive behaviors. If we worship Christ as the Creator, we desire to care for His creation. The human body is the most sacred of all that He has created. The Sabbath reminds us of Jesus' creative power and appeals to us to trust Him to remake us in His image.

The Sabbath reminds us of where we develop character—in a relationship with our heavenly Father and Jesus Christ. The Sabbath is a continual living promise of God's ability to help us grow through all of life's ups and downs, tragedies and triumphs. We need that distinctive time with the heavenly Father. We need quality Sabbath time with the God who sanctifies us—the God who helps us to keep growing.

The Sabbath has continued in the weekly cycle from the dawn of Creation until now. It began in the Garden of Eden, and the Sabbath will be celebrated when this earth is renewed after Christ's second coming. The prophet Isaiah speaks of the time when God will make "new heavens and the new earth" (Isaiah 66:22). He says:

> "And it shall come to pass
> That from one New Moon to another,
> And from one Sabbath to another,
> All flesh shall come to worship before Me," says the LORD (verse 23).

A forever relationship with God

The Sabbath beautifully represents a forever relationship with God. It stretches from the Garden of Eden at Creation to the garden that God will make of this planet at the end of time. It stretches from paradise lost to paradise restored. We need that kind of forever in our lives.

We need a place that reassures us that we are in an eternal relationship with the heavenly Father. We need a "palace in time"[2] where that assurance can sink in deep—a place that says our heavenly Father will always be there for us. In the Sabbath, we can find a sense of contented rest. We can get in touch with our roots as His children there. We can grow and mature there. Yes, we need that kind of forever place that ties the whole of our lives to an eternal relationship with God.

The message of three angels flying through the heavens, appealing for us to worship the Creator, is Heaven's answer to the hopeless despair of many in the twenty-first century. It is the answer to the dehumanizing philosophy of atheistic evolution. It is the answer to worry, tension, and fear. It is the answer to a lack of power and purpose. It is the answer to the hopelessness of our society because it points to Jesus—the God of today, tomorrow, and forever.

---

1. Joseph Mohr, "Silent Night, Holy Night" (1818).
2. Abraham Joshua Heschel, *The Sabbath* (New York: Farrar, Straus and Giroux, 2005), 14, 15.

9

A City Called Confusion

The founders of the United States clearly understood that if a church draws its authority and power from the state, intolerance and persecution often follow for those who do not conform to the church's mandates. These early American leaders were well acquainted with the tyranny of the state-church union in Europe. One of the reasons people left the Old World for the New was religious intolerance. Therefore, the founders wrote these memorable words into the First Amendment to the US Constitution: "Congress shall make no law respecting an establishment of religion, or prohibiting the free exercise thereof."[1]

George Washington, America's first president and a deeply religious man, stated: "I beg you will be persuaded that no one would be more zealous than myself to establish effectual barriers against the horrors of spiritual tyranny, and every species of religious persecution."[2]

Thomas Jefferson coined the expression "separation between church and state." By this, Jefferson meant that all people's religious convictions must be respected and that the government did not have the authority or right to establish a state religion or dictate the beliefs or nonbeliefs of its citizens.

Revelation 17 predicts that this will happen in the future under the auspices of spiritual Babylon. Verse 2 outlines this dramatic event: "The inhabitants of the earth were made drunk with the wine of her fornication."

The fallen church, described in Revelation 17:3, 4 as a woman dressed in purple and scarlet, sitting upon a scarlet-colored beast, influences the state to support her falsehoods (verses 3–6). She passes around her cup of erroneous doctrine. The world becomes intoxicated with these false religious ideas. Millions drink the wine of Babylon and are deceived. The Bible describes it this way in Revelation 17:3: "And I saw a woman sitting on a scarlet beast which was full of names of blasphemy, having seven heads and ten horns."

In Bible prophecy, a woman represents the church (Jeremiah 6:2). In Ephesians 5, a wife is likened to the church or the bride of Christ (verse 25). The woman in scarlet and purple in Revelation 17 is contrasted with the woman in white—the true followers of God—in Revelation 12:1. The harlot of Revelation 17 represents a false system of religion. Remember that in the Bible, a beast represents a king or a kingdom. Politicians, eager to retain their positions, will yield to the influence of the majority who have drunk the wine of Babylon's false doctrines. The apostate church's decrees will eventually be supported and enforced by the state. She derives power from the state but also influences the state. What a powerful symbol of an illicit union between church and state! One religious writer puts it this way: "The Church has . . . been able to gain outward recognition, and leaning on the worldly power—which in its turn makes use of the Church to achieve her own objects—she rules over the nations. Such is the picture of Christendom, ripe for judgment."[3]

When a nation turns its back on the principles of God's kingdom, it becomes beastlike. When the church leaves her true Lover, Jesus, and looks to the state for power and support, she compromises biblical principles and becomes the harlot.

Revelation 17:4 continues this intriguing drama: "The woman [remember, this is the harlot, the fallen church] was arrayed in purple and scarlet, and adorned with gold and precious stones and pearls." What colors does God use to describe this fallen system of religion that appeals to the state for its power? The colors are purple and scarlet. Do you know of a religious system whose religious leaders wear purple and scarlet vestments? In his book on the life of Constantine, the church historian Eusebius states, "In order to attach to Christianity greater attraction in the eyes of the nobility the [Catholic] priests adopted the outer garments and adornments which were used in pagan cults."[4]

Verse 4 continues: "In her hand [was] a golden cup full of abominations and the filthiness of her fornication." In the hand of this fallen system of religion, whose colors are purple and scarlet, is a cup, and all the world drinks from the cup and becomes confused by these false doctrines.

Now, where is the headquarters of this apostate religious system? "Here is the mind which has wisdom: The seven heads are seven mountains on which the woman sits" (verse 9).

Author and professor Ernest Martin makes this fascinating observation: "The fact that Rome was designated 'The Seven Hilled City' was significant enough to render it as a sacred and holy city that was designed to have world power and authority. This is one of the reasons the ancient people of the world always respected the City of Rome, whether they were its arch defenders and supporters or its enemies and were alien to its political and religious concepts."[5]

Let me be clear: there are other cities in the world built on seven hills, but there is only one—Rome—that meets all the identifying features in Revelation 17.

A City Called Confusion

Mystery, Babylon the Great

Now what name is on her forehead? Revelation 17:5 says,

And on her forehead a name was written:

MYSTERY, BABYLON THE GREAT,
THE MOTHER OF HARLOTS
AND OF THE ABOMINATIONS
OF THE EARTH.

The fallen system of religion outlined in Revelation 17 is called "Mystery, Babylon the Great." A review of the teachings of ancient spiritual Babylon will help us understand the falsehoods and errors that Satan has introduced into the Christian church. Philosopher George Santayana made this insightful statement: "Those who cannot remember the past are condemned to repeat it."[6]

In ancient Babylon, the world was commanded to bow in worship to a god of gold. Obedience to the commands of pagan religion was enforced through death decrees. The union of church and state in Babylon in the sixth century BC and its propagation of religious falsehoods that influenced all areas of life reveal how the devil will deceive multitudes in the future.

Now, if we can solve the mystery of Babylon the Great, we will understand the crucial significance of the symbolism of Revelation 17. What does the Bible mean when it says, "Mystery, Babylon the Great"? As we have already noted, by the first century AD, literal Babylon, the mighty empire that had dominated the Middle East, had already been destroyed. Once the Persian armies under Cyrus attacked and defeated Belshazzar, Babylon never rose to prominence again. Our passage cannot possibly be talking about *literal* Babylon, which had been destroyed for more than five hundred years by the time John wrote Revelation.

Revelation 17 is talking about *spiritual* Babylon—an apostate religious system that would depart from the pure teaching of God's Word and reintroduce many of the teachings of Old Testament Babylon to Christianity. This may sound amazing, but it is true. Sometimes truth is stranger than fiction. This prophecy is talking about a departure from the faith of Scripture. False doctrines would enter the church through this false religious system identified as Babylon the Great.

Babylon's falsehoods

In the Old Testament, a group of men and women rebelled against God shortly after the Flood by doubting His word. God had promised that there would never again be a worldwide flood. Disbelieving His word, they built a tower to reach into the heavens to protect themselves in the eventuality of another global catastrophe. The central issue was whether God can be trusted. Does He mean what He says?

The Tower of Babel was built in direct defiance of the word of God. The Babel builders substituted human ideas and man-made theories for clear instructions from Heaven. As they were building this monument for their own glory, God confused their languages. The Genesis account puts it this way: "Therefore its name is called Babel, because there the LORD confused the language of all the earth" (Genesis 11:9).

Lacking faith and refusing to hear what God said, they flagrantly violated the command of God. They turned from God's promise of protection to a human plan to protect themselves.

Babylon confused values

At this point, God confused the people's language. The city of Babylon was built on the site of the Tower of Babel. When you think of Babylon, think *confusion*. What are the first four letters in the word

A City Called Confusion

Babylon? *B-a-b-y*. Why do we call a baby a baby? We call a baby a baby because it babbles. A baby has confused speech, so it is a babbler. In the religious world, when religion becomes confused, truth becomes distorted, and human opinions are elevated above God's Word; it is nothing more than babbling—Babylon.

The book of Daniel is a companion book to Revelation. Describing the fundamental attitude of Babylonian philosophy, the prophet records the Babylonian king's arrogance in these words: "The king spoke, saying, 'Is not this great Babylon, that I have built for a royal dwelling by my mighty power and for the honor of my majesty?' " (Daniel 4:30).

Nebuchadnezzar, the Babylonian king, proudly boasted of his grand achievements in building the world-class city of Babylon. Catch the significance of this. Babylon is a man-made system. Spiritual Babylon represents a religion based on human teachings, established on human ideas, and supported by human traditions. There is a form of man-made religion that is built by brilliant human religious leaders, which stands in opposition to the power of the gospel and the truth of God's Word.

Jesus and His church

The message of Revelation portrays two systems of religion: one made by man and the other made by God. I have talked with some people who have said, "I believe that all religion is man made, and I do not want to have anything to do with organized churches." This thinking clearly contradicts Jesus' clear statement: "I will build My church, and the gates of Hades shall not prevail against it" (Matthew 16:18). This church has a solid foundation: Jesus Christ. It is built on the teachings of the Word of God and is guided by the Holy Spirit.

On the other hand, Babylon is a man-made system of religion. Jesus is calling us from all human systems of religion. He is calling us back to faithfulness to His Word. The church of Jesus Christ is not a man-made institution. The church of Jesus Christ was built by the Savior Himself. In fact, Colossians 1:18 states, "And He is the head of the body, the church, who is the beginning, the firstborn from the dead, that in all things He may have the preeminence."

Jesus Christ is the only Head of the church. The true church of God is the only organization so big that its body is upon Earth, but its Head is in heaven. Although Jesus guides His church through human leaders, their authority comes from His Word, not their human religious teachings. Any religious leader who substitutes or elevates human opinions or traditions in place of or above the revealed will of God in the Scriptures is simply fostering Babylonian confusion.

Babylon was the center of idolatry

Babylon was also the center of image worship. Idolatry was at the heart of Babylonian worship. The Babylonians believed that carved wooden or stone images were representations of their deities. Spiritual Babylon is a system of religion that emphasizes worshiping Christ, the virgin Mary, the apostles, and various so-called saints through images. It ascribes holiness and sacredness to these human creations.

Images limit the ability of the Holy Spirit to impress upon our minds the things of eternity. They are often given the sacredness and homage that belongs to God alone. We do not need to come to Jesus through the image of a saint. Jesus is our Intercessor. He is our Priest.

The Ten Commandments make this plain: "You shall not make for yourself a carved image—any likeness of anything that is in heaven above, or that is in the earth beneath, or that is in the water under the earth; you shall not bow down to them nor serve them. For I, the LORD your God, am a jealous God" (Exodus 20:4, 5).

Babylon used images prolifically in its worship services, and many of those images found their way from paganism to Rome and into the

Christian church. Erwin Goodenough, a professor of the history of religion, made this observation: "The Church did everything it could to stamp out such 'pagan' rites, but had to capitulate and allow the rites to continue with only the name of the local deity changed to some Christian saint's name."[7]

These images are still considered sacred today. Many represent the so-called saints who supposedly intercede for us before God.

The worship of images was also one of the major discussion points in the Protestant Reformation. The Catholic prelates argued that "the honor which is shown them [images] is referred to the prototypes which they represent, so that by means of the images which we kiss and before which we uncover the head and prostrate ourselves, we adore Christ and venerate the saints whose likeness they bear."[8]

Here is a forthright acknowledgment by the Roman hierarchy that the church instituted image worship. Their justification was that it was not the images that were worshiped but what they represented. This is similar to the thinking of the Babylonian system. The images of Babylon represented the Babylonian gods and were the vehicle through which to worship those gods. Tragically, millions of Christians revere images of so-called saints as objects of worship. This is one of Satan's deceptions to cloud their minds from the truth of God's Word.

In 1 Timothy 2:5, the apostle Paul states that "there is one God and one Mediator between God and men, the Man Christ Jesus." There is salvation in no other. Christ is the "image of the invisible God" (Colossians 1:15). We come to God through our mighty Intercessor, Jesus Christ.

In Acts 4, the apostle Peter was brought before the religious rulers in Jerusalem. He was condemned as a heretic, cast into prison, and brought to trial the next day. The Jewish leaders clothed salvation in the garb of legalism. Just as in building the ancient Tower of Babel, their good works became the means of their standing before God. Their acceptance with God was based on their behavior. Religion consisted of rituals, formalities, and duty.

Standing before the religious leaders of his day, Peter eloquently spoke of the salvation so freely provided in Christ: "Nor is there salvation in any other, for there is no other name under heaven given among men by which we must be saved" (verse 12).

There is only one way of salvation, and that is through the grace of Christ. Salvation does not come through man-made creeds. Salvation does not come through human religious institutions. Salvation does not come through religious pageantry, candles, incense, images, or rituals. Salvation comes only through Jesus Christ.

There is only One whose hands bear the prints of the nails. There is only One whose head wore the crown of thorns and whose back was lacerated with a Roman whip. There is only One who bled and died on a Roman cross for our salvation. There is only One who was placed in a freshly hewn rock tomb and was raised from the dead. There is only One who appears before the throne of God as our Intercessor. There is only One who is coming again in the clouds of heaven to take us home. His name is Jesus. Only Jesus can get us through the perilous times of the last days. Only Jesus can keep us from the deceptions of the evil one. Only Jesus can take us from here to eternity.

---

1. "First Amendment," Constitution Annotated, accessed September 19, 2022, https://constitution.congress.gov/browse/amendment-1/.

2. "From George Washington to the United Baptist Churches of Virginia, May 1789," Founders Online, accessed September 19, 2022, https://founders.archives.gov /documents/Washington/05-02-02-0309.

3. Karl Auberlen, *The Prophecies of Daniel and the Revelations of St John*, trans. Adolph Saphir (New York: Wiley and Halsted, 1857), 315.

4. Eusebius, *Life of Constantine*, cited in Nicholas Roerich, *Altai-Himalaya: A Travel Diary* (New York: Frederick A. Stokes, 1929), 94.

5. Ernest L. Martin, "The Seven Hills of Jerusalem," Associates for Scriptural Knowledge, February 1, 2000, https://www.askelm.com/prophecy/p000201.htm.

6. George Santayana, *Reason in Common Sense*, vol. 1 of *The Life of Reason*, 2nd ed. (New York: Charles Scribner's Sons, 1922), 284.

7. Erwin R. Goodenough, *Religious Tradition and Myth* (New Haven, CT: Yale University Press, 1937), 56, 57.

8. H. J. Schroeder, trans., *Canons and Decrees of the Council of Trent* (St. Louis, MO: B. Herder Book, 1960), 216. This discussion took place during the twenty-fifth session, on December 3, 4, 1563.

10

Satan's Final Deceptions

Belief in the supposed spirits of the dead played a significant role in the thinking of the ancient Babylonians. In fact, they believed that the disembodied spirit descended into the netherworld at death. The idea that there is an immortal soul that continues eternally after a person dies did not come from Christianity.

The concept of the immortality of the soul flows through the philosophies of ancient Egypt, Assyria, Babylon, and Greece. The Greeks popularized the idea of the immortal soul in the writings of Plato and Socrates. In Greek thought, the body was the prison house of the soul, and death liberated the soul from the body and allowed it to wing its way into the spirit world. However, the distinction between soul and body is at odds with the biblical view of death.

Here is one of the most incredible texts in the Bible, showing what can happen when God's people depart from the clear teachings of His Word: "And He said to me, 'Turn again, and you will see greater abominations that they are doing.' So He brought me to the door of the north gate of the LORD's house; and to my dismay, women were sitting there weeping for Tammuz" (Ezekiel 8:13, 14).

Who was Tammuz? Tammuz was the Mesopotamian god of fertility, embodying the powers of new life in nature in budding trees, blooming flowers, and lush vegetation. The Mesopotamians and the Babylonians believed that when winter darkened the sky and the nights were long, Tammuz had died. But in the spring, the power of Tammuz as an immortal deity lived on. Some of God's people, the Jews, accepted this false idea that derived from Babylon's confused theology.

That is why Ezekiel describes the women as worshiping Tammuz. They are worshiping the dead. This false idea that the dead live on and the soul is immortal slipped into Old Testament doctrine directly from paganism.

The truth about death
Here is what the Bible has to say about the truth of death:

> For the living know that they will die;
> But the dead know nothing,
> And they have no more reward,
> For the memory of them is forgotten (Ecclesiastes 9:5).

The living know they will die, but the dead do not know anything. The Bible's teaching on death could not be any clearer. The doctrine of the immortal soul is not in the Bible. This whole idea of the immortal soul comes from paganism.

Here is an excerpt from a sermon by biblical preacher Amos Phelps, who wrote these powerful words over 100 years ago in a chapter titled "Is Man by Nature Immortal?" He discusses the question of the immortality of the soul. He concludes: "This doctrine can be traced through the muddy channels of a corrupted Christianity, a perverted

Judaism, a pagan philosophy, and a superstitious idolatry, to the great instigator of mischief in the garden of Eden. The Protestants borrowed it from the Catholics, the Catholics from the Pharisees, the Pharisees from the Pagans, and the Pagans from the old Serpent, who first preached the doctrine amid the lovely bowers of Paradise to an audience all too willing to hear and heed the new and fascinating theology—'Ye shall not surely die.' "[1]

What did Satan say to Eve in the Garden of Eden? He essentially said, "Eve, you are immortal." The first great deception in the Garden of Eden was closely aligned with Satan's appeal for her to disobey an express command of God.

Just as Satan deceived Eve through his spiritualistic manifestation of using the serpent as a medium, he will work through his evil spirits to deceive multitudes today. Just before the coming of Jesus, Satan will work with all of his power to deceive. Revelation 16:14 describes his final deception this way: "For they are spirits of demons, performing signs, which go out to the kings of the earth and of the whole world, to gather them to the battle of that great day of God Almighty."

Satan brings about the final union of church and state through spiritualistic deceptions. The idea of the immortality of the soul gave way to the pagan rituals of offerings for the dead, worshiping the dead, and bowing before images supposedly representing the dead. It gave way to the Christian doctrine of saints (supposedly departed loved ones) who are said to be hovering around us, desiring to communicate with us. It will also pave the way for the last deception of Satan in his attempt to control this planet.

The three angels' messages warn us against this last-day deception by revealing the truth about death. Revelation 14:13 declares,

" 'Blessed are the dead who die in the Lord from now on.' "

"Yes," says the Spirit, "that they may rest from their labors, and their works follow them."

In Scripture, death is a rest—a sleep until the return of our Lord. You see, the idea of the immortality of the soul greatly diminishes the doctrine of the second coming of Christ. It strikes at the very heart of Christianity. If you believe in the immortality of the soul, you may also logically believe that you immediately go to heaven when you die. So why then would Jesus come to resurrect the dead if they were already in heaven? This false teaching undercuts the second coming of Christ.

God intended that the church in every age would long for the second coming of Christ. The apostle Paul plainly states in 1 Thessalonians 4:16, 17, "For the Lord Himself will descend from heaven with a shout, with the voice of an archangel, and with the trumpet of God. And the dead in Christ will rise first. Then we who are alive and remain shall be caught up together with them in the clouds to meet the Lord in the air. And thus we shall always be with the Lord." According to the Bible, our loved ones rest in Jesus until His second coming. When Jesus returns, together with them, we will be caught up to meet Jesus in the air.

Is it possible that a misunderstanding of this truth explains why so many churches are spiritually dead? Could it explain their lack of spiritual power? The truth is, they have lost the urgency of the second coming of Christ. They have lost their passion for Jesus' return. I thank God that the Bible leads us to the realization that Jesus Christ is coming, and He is coming soon. And our hearts can beat with the eager anticipation that our dead loved ones who died longing for the return of their Lord will be resurrected to meet Christ in the sky.

The immortality of the soul—a Babylonian deception—is a false understanding of death that opens the way for the deceitful influence of spiritualism. The next great deception focuses specifically on worship.

Babylon was also the center of sun worship

Sun worship was prominent in Egypt, Assyria, Persia, and certainly Babylon. In his book *The Worship of Nature*, James G. Frazer observes, "In ancient Babylonia the Sun was worshipped from immemorial antiquity."[2] Babylonian sun worship impacted the people of God. Ezekiel, a contemporary of Daniel, wrote about the influence of Babylonian sun worship on some worshipers in Judea. "He brought me into the inner court of the LORD's house; and there, at the door of the temple of the LORD, between the porch and the altar, were about twenty-five men with their backs toward the temple of the LORD and their faces toward the east, and they were worshiping the sun toward the east" (Ezekiel 8:16).

Here is a fascinating bit of history that helps us understand the origin of Sunday worship. Satan has attempted to exalt the creation above the Creator in every generation. He is the master deceiver. He tries to get people to worship the objects of creation rather than the One who created those objects. He has attempted to counterfeit the truth of Scripture with falsehoods.

As we have discovered, some Jews accepted the Babylonian idea that the soul was immortal, so they were praying to Tammuz. But they were doing something else in the inner court of the Lord's house. What was it? Here it is: there "were about twenty-five men with their backs toward the temple of the LORD and their faces toward the east, and they were worshiping the sun toward the east."

When these worshipers came to the temple, they did not turn their backs to the east, as was customary, but faced the east to worship the sun. This, of course, was a pagan practice directly from Babylon.

In Revelation 14 and 17, John describes a time when the principles of Babylon, including sun worship, would slip into the Christian church during an age of compromise. Author John Eadie gives us this insight: "*Sunday* was a name given by the heathen to the first day of the week, because it was the day on which they worshipped the sun."[3] The day of the sun was a popular pagan holiday.

The casual conversion of Constantine in the early part of the fourth century AD caused great joy in the Roman Empire, but under a religious guise, the world, cloaked with a form of righteousness, walked into the church. Constantine had a strong affinity for sun worship. Renowned historian Edward Gibbon wrote, "The sun was universally celebrated as the invincible guide and protector of Constantine."[4]

In AD 321, Constantine passed the first Sunday law in an attempt to unite his empire during social upheaval. He issued an edict, stating, "On the venerable Day of the Sun let the magistrates and people residing in the cities rest, and let all workshops be closed."[5]

The significance of this law cannot be overstated. It was not a law enforcing Sunday observance for all of Constantine's subjects, but it did strengthen the observance of Sunday in the minds of the entire Roman population.

In succeeding decades, emperors and popes continued to establish Sunday as the day of worship through state decrees and church councils. Here is a quote from *Catholic World* on the same subject: "The sun was a foremost god with heathendom. . . . Hence the church in these countries would seem to have said, 'Keep that old, pagan name. It shall remain consecrated, sanctified.' And thus the pagan Sunday, dedicated to Balder, became the Christian Sunday, sacred to Jesus."[6]

Truth will overcome deception

Even for the casual observer of church history, it is evident that pagan practices have crept into the Christian church. Teachings from ancient Babylon have influenced most Christian churches. When the

Protestant churches protested some of these practices, they did not protest enough. They left the mother church of Rome, but they did not go far enough.

During the Protestant Reformation, God raised up great men and women of faith, but unfortunately, they retained some of the errors from the mother church. The immortality of the soul and Sunday worship are just two examples of the falsehoods the great deceiver has led multitudes to accept. The messages of Revelation 14 and 17 warn all committed believers to recognize that falsehoods will enter the Christian church again. They are an appeal from Jesus Himself so that we will understand the momentous events soon to burst upon this world as an overwhelming surprise.

The good news is that God has millions of honest-hearted men and women who love Him and long to know His truth. Their hearts respond as they study God's Word and learn new truths. All they want is what God wants. They are amazed that more religious leaders are not teaching the fullness of God's truth from His Word.

In the days of Ezekiel, when error slipped in among the people of God, He cried out, "Her priests have violated My law and profaned My holy things; they have not distinguished between the holy and unholy, nor have they made known the difference between the unclean and the clean; and they have hidden their eyes from My Sabbaths, so that I am profaned among them" (Ezekiel 22:26).

It is likely that if the prophet Ezekiel were alive today, God's message would still be same. John the revelator echoes these same thoughts in Revelation 14, 17, and 18. The voice from heaven makes an urgent appeal for honest-hearted people in Babylon—the apostate churches teaching contrary to biblical teachings—to "come out of her, my people" (Revelation 18:4). If the apostle John were alive today, he would cry out for people to flee from the errors that have become part of a fallen church system called spiritual Babylon.

Satan's Final Deceptions

Soon this world will be confronted with Satan's greatest deception. Through the twin errors of Sunday sacredness and the immortality of the soul, he will attempt to unite the religious world. Once again church and state will unite, and religious intolerance will follow. Speaking with penetrating insight, Ellen White states:

> Through the two great errors, the immortality of the soul and Sunday sacredness, Satan will bring the people under his deceptions. While the former lays the foundation of spiritualism, the latter creates a bond of sympathy with Rome. The Protestants of the United States will be foremost in stretching their hands across the gulf to grasp the hand of spiritualism; they will reach over the abyss to clasp hands with the Roman power; and under the influence of this threefold union, this country will follow in the steps of Rome in trampling on the rights of conscience.[7]

The message of the second angel in Revelation 14 is "Babylon is fallen, is fallen" (verse 8). In Revelation 17, the woman identified as spiritual Babylon, dressed in purple and scarlet, rides upon a scarlet-colored beast, passing around her cup and getting the world drunk with error. Church and state unite. Falsehood prevails. Demons work their miracles to deceive. The world catapults into its final conflict. The people of God are maligned, ridiculed, oppressed, and persecuted, but in Christ and through the power of His Holy Spirit, they are steadfast in their commitment. All the powers of hell and the forces of evil cannot break their loyalty to Christ. They are secure in Him. He is their "refuge and strength"—a "very present help in trouble" (Psalm 46:1).

1. Amos Phelps, "Is Man by Nature Immortal?", in *The Life Everlasting*, ed. J. H. Pettingell, 2nd ed. (Philadelphia: J. D. Brown, 1883), 640, 641.

2. James G. Frazer, *The Worship of Nature*, vol. 1 (New York: Macmillan, 1926), 529.

3. *A Biblical Cyclopædia*, ed. John Eadie, 13th ed. (London: Charles Griffin, 1872), s.v. "Sabbath" (561); emphasis in the original.

4. Edward Gibbon, *The History of the Decline and Fall of the Roman Empire*, vol. 1 (New York: J. & J. Harper, 1831), 413.

5. Philip Schaff, *History of the Christian Church*, vol. 3, 3rd ed. (New York: Charles Scribner's Sons, 1889), 380n1.

6. William L. Gildea, "Paschale Gaudium," *Catholic World*, March 1894, 809.

7. Ellen G. White, *The Great Controversy* (Nampa, ID: Pacific Press®, 2002), 588.

11

The Seal of God and the Mark of the Beast: Part 1

The message of the book of Revelation is much more than cryptic symbols, strange beasts, and odd images. It speaks of eternal truths written by a loving God to an end-time generation.

The central issue in Earth's final conflict has to do with worship. The conflict between Christ and Satan over the issue of worship began in heaven and will reach its final climax at the close of Earth's history.

Let us review three passages in Revelation 14 that establish this point. The messages we have been studying are so important that they are pictured as being carried by three angels flying swiftly through the sky.

In Revelation 14:7, the first angel cries with a loud voice: "Fear God and give glory to Him, for the hour of His judgment has come; and worship Him who made heaven and earth, the sea and springs of water." This is Heaven's appeal to give our supreme allegiance and heartfelt worship to the Creator in light of Heaven's cosmic judgment.

In Revelation 14:8, a second angel declares, "Babylon is fallen, is fallen, that great city, because she has made all nations drink of the wine of the wrath of her fornication." As we have studied in the two previous chapters, Babylon represents an apostate religious system that has substituted falsehood for truth. She has rejected the first angel's message, so the second angel's message announces that she has fallen from God's favor.

In Revelation 14:9, 10, the third angel warns against worshiping the beast. The angel declares in trumpeting tones: "If anyone worships the beast and his image, and receives his mark on his forehead or on his hand, he himself shall also drink of the wine of the wrath of God."

Revelation 14:12 summarizes the issues this way: "Here is the patience [endurance] of the saints [believers]; here are those who keep the commandments of God and the faith of Jesus." God will have an end-time people loyal to Him in the face of the greatest opposition and fiercest persecution in the history of the world. Lovingly and loyally, they will live God-centered, grace-filled, and obedient lives. Worshiping the Creator stands in direct opposition to worshiping the beast and finds its expression in keeping the commandments of God.

The Sabbath, of course, is the sign of Christ's creative authority. This final conflict over allegiance to Christ versus loyalty to the beast power centers on worship, and at the heart of this great controversy between good and evil is the Sabbath. The committed followers of the Savior will not only have faith *in* Jesus but also have the faith *of* Jesus. Jesus' quality of end-time faith will be theirs. Hanging on the cross, enshrouded in darkness, bearing the guilt, shame, and condemnation of the sins of the world, seemingly shut off from His Father's love, Jesus depended on the relationship He had shared with the Father throughout His life. To rely on His emotions would have been an absolute spiritual disaster. The Savior trusted, even when He could not discern the future. He believed when there was little evidence for belief. He had faith when, all around Him, the circumstances cried out for Him to doubt.

The faith of Jesus is so deep, trusting, and committed that all the demons in hell and all the trials on Earth could not shake it. It is a faith that trusts when it cannot see, believes when it cannot understand, hopes when it cannot comprehend, and hangs on when there is little to hang on to. This faith of Jesus is itself a gift that we receive by faith and will carry us through the troubles ahead. In this final crisis, when the faithful followers of Christ will face an economic boycott, will be unable to buy or sell, and will be threatened with persecution, the faith of Jesus will carry them through the trials and tribulations of Earth's final hours.

Throughout Revelation, worship and creation are indissolubly linked. Revelation 14:7 calls us to worship the Lord of all creation. The essence of this controversy between good and evil and the issues surrounding the mark of the beast revolve around whether God is worthy to be worshiped. The focus is on the God of all creation.

The concept of Christ as Creator is at the very heart of Sabbath worship. Jesus consistently underlines the significance of the day of which He calls Himself "Lord" (Matthew 12:8; Mark 2:28; Luke 6:5). We then see the Sabbath in the context of a refuge in time that God has created through Jesus Christ to remind us of our origins and His undying care. It is an oasis in the desert of this world. Against the backdrop of the evolution hypothesis that has taken the world by storm in the last two centuries, the Sabbath leads us back to our roots. The Sabbath is an eternal reminder of our identity. It reminds us of who we are as humans. It places worth on every human being. It constantly reinforces the idea that we are created beings and that our Creator is worthy of our allegiance and worship. This is why the devil hates the Sabbath so much. It is the golden link that unites us with our Creator.

Trouble ahead

In Revelation 13, the beast targets God's people by seeking to fracture the Sabbath link. Ever since Jesus died on the cross, the enemy has known that he has been defeated, but he is determined to take as many as possible down with him. His first strategy in this campaign is deception and getting people to believe a lie. In this, he has achieved huge success. But still, there are some holdouts. The prophecy of the mark of the beast tells about a time in the future when he will resort to force. He will use human agents, as he always has, and will convince them to issue a decree, stating that anyone who refuses to worship the beast or receive his mark will suffer the consequences.

Religious persecution, of course, is not new. It has been around since Cain killed Abel for worshiping the way God told them to. Jesus said it would even happen among believers. "The time is coming," He warned, "that whoever kills you will think that he offers God service" (John 16:2; see also Matthew 10:22; 1 Peter 4:12). This prophecy has been fulfilled many times. In the fifteenth century, for example, seven valleys high in the Piedmont region of the Alps of northern Italy were home to the Waldenses, who made the Bible their rule of faith and practice. They copied the Scriptures and sent out their young men as colporteurs to spread the good news that salvation is a gift of God's love.

Because of this, and because they rejected the doctrines and the authority of the official church, the fires of persecution blazed against them. In 1488, the Waldenses in the valley of Loyse hid in a large cave to escape the soldiers sent to slaughter them. It seemed like a safe place, but their enemies laid an enormous pile of wood at the mouth of the cave and set it ablaze. Three thousand men, women, and children died that day from smoke and suffocation.

Another wave of persecution came in the seventeenth century when the Duke of Savoy sent an army of eight thousand into their territory and demanded that the local populace quarter his troops in their homes. They did as he requested, but this was a strategy to give the soldiers easy access to their victims. On April 24, 1655, at 4:00 A.M., a signal was given for the massacre to begin. Men, women, children, and the elderly were targeted. Parents were forced to watch as their children were sexually violated and then murdered before they themselves were put to death. The death toll on this occasion was more than four thousand.

The prophecy of the mark of the beast is the final link in this ungodly chain. Like past persecutions, it is designed to force everyone to conform to a specific set of beliefs and an approved system of worship. The prophecy says the persecution will start with economic sanctions: "no one may buy or sell" unless they have "the mark" (Revelation 13:17). When this happens, the great majority will capitulate. Anyone who refuses will be placed under a death decree (verse 15). Ellen White observes that those who yield their conscientious convictions will ultimately receive the mark of the beast: "The time is not far distant when the test will come to every soul. The mark of the beast will be urged upon us. Those who have step by step yielded to worldly demands and conformed to worldly customs will not find it a hard matter to yield to the powers that be, rather than subject themselves to derision, insult, threatened imprisonment, and death."[1]

The devil is preparing even professed Christians, by compromises in their lives, to receive the mark of the beast when the final test comes upon us in the future. God's love for each of us will not let us go unprepared. This is why He has sent three angels directly from His throne, flying in midheaven to warn us regarding what is coming.

Satan uses force and coercion

The book of Revelation reveals God's plans and unmasks Satan's plans. It tells us in advance what the devil's strategy is. Let us zero in on this final conflict, and let Bible prophecy and history identify the beast and his mark. As we understand who the beast of Bible prophecy is and what the mark of the beast is, we will better understand the opposite sign—the seal of God. Revelation gives us some clear identifying clues to recognize the beast.

Notice Revelation 13: "Then I [John] stood on the sand of the sea. And I saw a beast rising up out of the sea, having seven heads and ten horns, and on his horns ten crowns, and on his heads a blasphemous name. Now the beast which I saw was like a leopard, his feet were like the feet of a bear, and his mouth like the mouth of a lion. The dragon gave him his power, his throne, and great authority" (verses 1, 2).

The beast power of Revelation 13 receives his power from the dragon. Who is the dragon? Revelation 12:9 identifies the dragon plainly: "So the great dragon was cast out, that serpent of old, called the Devil and Satan, who deceives the whole world; he was cast to the earth, and his angels were cast out with him." The dragon is clearly identified in this verse. In simple language stripped of all symbolism, God's Word tells us that the dragon is the devil—Satan. The archenemy of God and man is behind the human instrumentality called the beast power.

But the devil works through *human* agents. Just as God works through His church, the devil works through fallen religious institutions that have rejected God's truth and turned their backs on His law. Revelation 12:3–5 says this dragon—the devil—attempted to destroy, as soon as He was born, the male Child who was later "caught up to God and His throne." This Child, of course, refers to Christ. Satan used pagan Rome in this attempt; Matthew 2:1–20 tells us that King Herod, Rome's agent, tried to destroy Jesus at His birth. This wicked king issued a decree that all male children born in Bethlehem under two years of age were to be killed.

Later, Satan used pagan Rome to crucify Christ. A Roman governor, Pilate, condemned Jesus to die. A Roman executioner nailed Him to the cruel cross. A Roman soldier pierced His side with a spear. A Roman seal was affixed to His tomb. And a Roman squad of soldiers guarded the tomb.

Whoever this beast power is, Revelation 13:2 says, "The dragon gave him his power, his throne, and great authority." This prophecy was fulfilled precisely when the Roman emperor Constantine decided to move the imperial capital from Rome to what came to be called Constantinople (today called Istanbul), in modern-day Turkey, leaving a power vacuum at the former throne or seat of the Caesars—the city of Rome. Through the centuries, careful Bible students have identified Rome as the citadel of the beast power.

The dragon—the devil—working through pagan Rome, tried to destroy Christ. And that same power, pagan Rome, gave the beast its seat or capital city. Nations do not do that very often!

To whom did pagan Rome give its seat of government? How did this transition take place? Historian Alexander C. Flick explains that "out of the ruins of political Rome, arose the great moral Empire in the 'giant form' of the Roman Church."[2] English philosopher and historian Thomas Hobbes wrote that "the Papacy is no other than the ghost of the deceased Roman empire, sitting crowned upon the grave thereof."[3]

The papal system of religion is the one mentioned in Revelation 13. We must remember here that we are talking about a system, not about individual members of that system. The beast is not a person but a religious organization that has compromised the truth of God's Word for human tradition.

John the revelator continues his description:

And I saw one of his [the beast's] heads as if it had been mortally wounded, and his deadly wound was healed. And all the world marveled and followed the beast. So they worshiped the dragon who gave authority to the beast; and they worshiped the beast, saying, "Who is like the beast? Who is able to make war with him?"

And he was given a mouth speaking great things and blasphemies, and he was given authority to continue for forty-two months (Revelation 13:3–5).

According to a careful analysis of Revelation's identifying features, the beast of Revelation 13 and 14 is an apostate religious power that rose out of Rome and grew to become a worldwide system of worship. This system of worship would supplant the worship of God. It would urge people to worship on a man-made day of worship rather than on the seventh-day Sabbath.

Millennia ago, a created being—an angel of dazzling brightness—challenged the government of God in heaven. God gave each of His creatures free will. Our God is a God of freedom. Love is the great motivating force of the kingdom of God. But the beast uses force and coercion and, at times, bribes and rewards. This agelong drama, this cosmic conflict, will one day come to its conclusion, and the universe will be secure forever when every person on planet Earth has had the opportunity to respond to God's love and give their allegiance to Him.

The cross of Calvary revealed the horrible nature of sin and the magnificence of God's love. Rather than worship the beast, God's people find their greatest joy and highest delight in worshiping Him. They are willing to do whatever He asks because they know He will never harm them; obedience springs from their hearts of love. They are committed to Him because they know He is committed to them.

Only one thing will keep us from receiving the mark of the beast at the end, and that is a love for Jesus that is so deep that nothing can break our hold upon Him.

Will you commit your life to this Christ today? Will you ask Him to give you a love for Him that is so strong that all the demons of hell cannot cause you to yield your conscientious convictions? Will you open your heart to His grace and power that will enable you to stand in Earth's last days?

---

1. Ellen G. White, *Testimonies for the Church* (Mountain View, CA: Pacific Press®, 1948), 5:81.

2. Alexander C. Flick, *The Rise of the Mediæval Church* (New York: Burt Franklin, 1909), 150.

3. William Molesworth, ed., *Leviathan*, vol. 3 of *The English Works of Thomas Hobbes of Malmesbury* (London: John Bohn, 1839), 697, 698.

12

The Seal of God and the Mark of the Beast: Part 2

As we journey through Revelation's three cosmic messages, this chapter continues our investigation of the mark of the beast and the seal of God. Let us summarize what we have previously discovered. We saw that the final conflict in the agelong controversy between good and evil is over worship. A rebel angel has challenged the government of God. This being of dazzling brightness, created with free will, has declared that God is unjust. He claims that God's commands are arbitrary and cannot be obeyed. In every generation, the evil one has led men and women to disobey God. In the last days, God demonstrates that His gracious commands are for our best good. Saved by grace and redeemed by love, Christ's faithful followers willingly serve Him because they know His ways are the ways of lasting joy.

Finally, Satan will attempt to pull off his greatest delusion of all time in a religious counterfeit called the beast power. We noted previously that this power would arise in Rome and become a world-wide system of worship. Let us continue with further clues to the identity of this power and discover essential truths about the coming conflict in the last days of Earth's history.

Throughout the book of Revelation, the apostate church is described as a blasphemous power. In Revelation 13:1, we find the expression "on his heads a blasphemous name." Verse 6 states, "Then he opened his mouth in blasphemy against God, to blaspheme His name, His tabernacle, and those who dwell in heaven." And in Revelation 17:3: "So he carried me away in the Spirit into the wilderness. And I saw a woman sitting on a scarlet beast which was full of names of blasphemy, having seven heads and ten horns."

Blasphemy

Since blasphemy is mentioned numerous times as one of the identifying features of the beast power, it must be significant. Let us discover how this term is used in other places in the New Testament. On more than one occasion, Jesus was called a blasphemer. In John 10:33, the Jewish leaders charged Him with blasphemy: "The Jews answered Him, saying, 'For a good work we do not stone You, but for blasphemy, and because You, being a Man, make Yourself God.' " Notice carefully that the religious leaders of Jesus' day claimed He was a blasphemer because He claimed to be God. Was Jesus a blasphemer? Certainly not! Why not? Simply because His claims were true. This passage helps us to understand the biblical meaning of blasphemy.

When a mortal person claims God's privileges and prerogatives as an equal, that is blasphemy. But there is another incident in Jesus' life that casts light on what blasphemy is. Shortly after Jesus forgave the sins of a desperate paralytic, "the scribes and the Pharisees began to reason, saying, 'Who is this who speaks blasphemies? Who can forgive sins but God alone?' " (Luke 5:21).

These are two occasions when the Lord Jesus was accused of blasphemy. They give us two biblical examples of blasphemy: (1) a person pretends to be or claims to be God, and (2) a person claims the power to forgive sins. In Jesus' case, the accusations were unjust because He truly was and is God and holds all the powers and prerogatives of God—including the right to forgive our sins.

Now that we understand the biblical definition of blasphemy, let us discover how blasphemy was revealed in the apostate church of the Middle Ages. The Roman Catholic Church has two distinctive doctrines identified in the Bible as blasphemy. One is its priests claim to have the power to forgive sins. The second is attributing to the pope the office of God on Earth. We will examine each of these.

The Roman Church claims that the power of forgiveness of sins, or absolution, is vested in her priests by Christ Himself. Here is a very pointed statement from a prominent Catholic author: "Seek where you will, throughout heaven and earth, and you will find but one created being who can forgive the sinner, who can free him from the chains of sin and hell: and that extraordinary being is the priest, the Catholic priest. 'Who can forgive sins except God?' was the question which the Pharisees sneeringly asked. 'Who can forgive sins?' is the question which the Pharisees of the present day also ask, and I answer: There is a man on earth that can forgive sins, and that man is the Catholic priest."[1]

In 1 Timothy 2:5, the Bible teaches that there is but "one Mediator between God and men, the Man Jesus Christ." The Roman Church teaches that the priest is the mediator between God and sinful humanity. But since the priest himself is a sinful human being, he cannot be our mediator because he also needs a mediator.

The official teaching of the Roman Church is that God dispenses the grace of forgiveness through the priest. Proof of the church's teaching of this doctrine is seen in a news item under the following headline: "No Forgiveness 'Directly From God,' Pope Says."[2] This is a shocking statement in light of the clear Bible truth: "If we confess our sins, He is faithful and just to forgive us our sins and to cleanse us from all unrighteousness" (1 John 1:9).

Jesus' sacrifice on the cross was complete. However, the atonement He provided on the cross is applied to individual lives through His intercession in the heavenly sanctuary. We need a sacrifice—Jesus. We need a priest—Jesus. Earthly priests can never substitute for the divine Priest. The earthly sacrifice of the Mass can never substitute for the atonement provided by Christ.[3]

By faith, we see the heavenly sanctuary where Jesus ministers. Our eyes are not focused on an earthly sanctuary with its incense, candles, priests, and sacrifice of the Mass because we are focused on heaven's sanctuary. It is there in heaven, before the throne of God, that Jesus intercedes for us before the entire universe. All of this is vital background to understanding Revelation 13.

Now we turn to our second biblical example, concerning any person's claim to be God or to stand in the place of God. Here are just a few statements from authoritative Catholic sources:

The Pope is of so great dignity and so exalted that he is not a mere man, but as it were God, and the vicar of God. . . .

Hence the Pope is crowned with a triple crown, as king of heaven and of earth and of the lower regions. . . .

The Pope is as it were God on earth, sole sovereign of the faithful of Christ, chief king of kings, . . . to whom has been intrusted by the omnipotent God direction not only of the earthly but also of the heavenly kingdom.[4]

Pope Leo XIII urged "complete submission and obedience of will to the Church and to the Roman Pontiff, as to God Himself."[5] The same proud pontiff also boasted: "We [the popes] hold upon this earth the place of God Almighty."[6]

Three Cosmic Messages

More evidence could be given, but these two admissions are enough to establish the claims of the Roman Church that the pope stands in the place of God Himself. The apostle Paul warns us in 2 Thessalonians 2:3, 4: "Let no one deceive you by any means; for that Day [Christ's second coming] will not come unless the falling away [from the truth] comes first, and the man of sin is revealed, the son of perdition, who opposes and exalts himself above all that is called God or that is worshiped, so that he sits as God in the temple of God, showing himself that he is God."

Although multiple authors wrote the Bible, it is a unified whole. It employs a variety of symbols, all pointing to the same conclusion: the Roman Church is the beast power of Revelation 13 and 14.

The Bible teaches that if any mere human being claims to be God, that person has committed an act of blasphemy. We also find that an earthly religious leader who claims the ability to forgive our sins has committed blasphemy. Such a leader usurps the authority that belongs to God alone.

So far in our study, we have discovered that the beast power of Revelation 13 and 14 is a worldwide system of worship that receives the seat of its government and its throne from pagan Rome. Its leader claims the authority of God, and its priests claim the divine right to forgive sins.

There is another crucial identifying sign of the beast power in Revelation 13:5: "And he [the beast power] was given a mouth speaking great things and blasphemies, and he was given authority to continue for forty-two months."

The beast would continue for a period with a specific duration. Keep in mind a crucial scriptural principle as we study this clue. In symbolic time prophecies, a prophetic day equals a literal year. This principle has proven itself repeatedly in actual practice. Calculating the actual time period mentioned in Revelation 13:5 of forty-two months, with thirty days in a month as used in Bible times, we come up with 1,260 prophetic days or literal years.

Sunday worship

These 1,260 years encompass the dominance of the medieval church. The Roman Church gained growing power in the fourth and fifth centuries after Christ. The Roman emperor Constantine legalized Christianity throughout the empire. When he moved his capital in AD 330 to what became known as Constantinople, uniting the eastern and western parts of his empire, it left a leadership vacuum in Rome. The pope then filled this void and became not only a powerful religious leader but also a political force to be reckoned with in Europe. In AD 538, Justinian, the Roman emperor, officially granted the Roman bishop the role of defender of the faith, definer of heretics, and arbiter of truth. The papacy exercised great influence from AD 538 throughout the Middle Ages. At the end of the 1,260 years, Napoleon's General Berthier took the pope captive in 1798—exactly on time.

This act of General Berthier fulfilled Revelation's prophecy: "He who leads into captivity shall go into captivity" (Revelation 13:10). Berthier and his army captured Pope Pius VI and unceremoniously removed him from the papal throne. The aged pontiff was hurried from prison to prison and confined, at length, in a fortress near the Alps. He was later removed to Valence, France, where, in 1799, he died alone and in exile.

The blow to the papacy was serious but not fatal. According to the prediction in Revelation 13:12, the "deadly wound" would be healed. The stature of the papacy would increase, and its influence would once again be felt worldwide. Today, the Roman pontiff is gaining authority, power, and influence worldwide. World leaders welcome the pope as he travels around the world as an ambassador of the Church of Rome.

For example, the pope was warmly welcomed at the United Nations in 2015 when he toured the United States. He was invited to address a joint session of the US Congress in a move that many political observers considered unprecedented. Kings, presidents, political leaders, and dignitaries visit him regularly at the Vatican and treat him as royalty when he visits their countries. By all external appearances, the papacy seems to be softening its image to accommodate the spirit of our age. At a time when the world is looking for moral leadership, the pope's star is rising rapidly.

Have you ever wondered what the devil might use to unify society? History often repeats itself, so let us return momentarily to the days of Constantine. The Roman Empire was falling apart. The Germanic invasions from the north were ravaging western Europe. The barbarian tribes were overthrowing cities and towns throughout the Roman Empire. In an attempt to save his empire, Constantine turned to religion. The authority of the church, combined with the power of the state, became the very instrument Constantine was searching for.

Constantine wanted his empire united, and the Roman Church wanted it converted. This is why Constantine passed the first Sunday law, and the church reinforced his decree in church councils by making Sunday the sacred day of worship. The renowned historian Arthur Weigall states it clearly: "The Church made a sacred day of Sunday . . . largely because it was the weekly festival of the sun; for it was a definite Christian policy to take over the pagan festivals endeared to the people by tradition, and to give them a Christian significance."[7]

A common day of worship has the potential to unite a divided world. The issue of the mark of the beast revolves around worship. It focuses on the issue of authority. Since the change of the Bible Sabbath was instituted by a church-state union in the early Christian church, worship on the first day of the week is the sign of papal authority. To change the law of God, someone or some group must have authority that is (falsely) assumed to be higher than God's authority.

Make no mistake about it: the day is coming—and possibly sooner than we think—when laws will be passed restricting our religious liberty. Those who conscientiously follow the Word of God and keep the true Sabbath of the Lord will be labeled as opposing unity and the good of society. Ellen White clarifies these issues in the book *The Great Controversy*: "Those who honor the Bible Sabbath will be denounced as enemies of law and order, as breaking down the moral restraints of society, causing anarchy and corruption, and calling down the judgments of God upon the earth. Their conscientious scruples will be pronounced obstinacy, stubbornness, and contempt of authority. They will be accused of disaffection toward the government."[8] "As the movement for Sunday enforcement becomes more bold and decided, the law will be invoked against commandment keepers. They will be threatened with fines and imprisonment, and some will be offered positions of influence, and other rewards and advantages, as inducements to renounce their faith."[9]

Sealed for eternity

In this time of crisis, God's faithful people will, by His grace and through His power, stand firm in their convictions to follow Him. They heed Christ's command in John 14:15: "If you love Me, keep My commandments." They have not yielded to the pressure and coercion of the beast power. They are sealed with the seal of the Holy Spirit and cannot be moved. Revelation 7:2 depicts an angel "ascending from the east, having the seal of the living God." This angel cries with a loud voice, "Do not harm the earth, the sea, or the trees till we have sealed the servants of God on their foreheads" (verse 3).

The prophecy of Revelation 13 tells us that in the last days, during the time of universal crisis, God's people step forward and place their stamp—their seal—on the covenant by keeping the Sabbath. When they do this, it will be God's turn. Then He will step forward and place His stamp—His seal of approval—on them. This is His guarantee, His ratification given in the sight of the universe, showing that these are, indeed, His true followers.

God wants the universe to behold the triumph of His grace in these people. He wants everyone to know that even in the time of universal apostasy and repudiation of His law—yes, even in the face of a death decree—He will have a people whose loyalty to Him is unswerving. The sealing is God's shout of triumph and His victory banner that He will wave before the universe.

The hearts of believers, saved by grace, are filled with the faith of Jesus. His faith motivates and changes them. It inspires and empowers them. It frees them from the guilt of the past, delivers them from the bondage of sin in the present, and fills them with hope for the future. Saved by grace, they can do nothing else but, through His power, give Him their allegiance and serve and obey Him forever.

---

1. Michael Müller, *God the Teacher of Mankind*, vol. 6 (New York: Benziger Brothers, 1882), 332.

2. Don A. Schanche, "No Forgiveness 'Directly From God,' Pope Says," *Los Angeles Times*, December 12, 1984, 11.

3. Portions of this chapter are adapted from Mark Finley, "The Mark of the Beast," interview by Bill Knott, *Adventist Review*, June 1, 2018, https://adventistreview.org/magazine-article/the-mark-of-the-beast/.

4. Lucii Ferraris, *Prompta Bibliotheca canonica, juridica, moralis, theologica*, vol. 5 (Paris: Jacques-Paul Migne, 1854), 1791–1864, translated and quoted in Carlyle B. Haynes, "The Great Counterfeit of Christianity," *Protestant Magazine*, October 1915, 492.

5. Leo XIII, *Sapientiae Christiane* (*On Christians as Citizens*), encyclical letter, Vatican, January 10, 1890, https://www.vatican.va/content/leo-xiii/en/encyclicals/documents/hf_l-xiii_enc_10011890_sapientiae-christianae.html.

6. Leo XIII, *Praeclara Gratulationis Publicae* (*The Reunion of Christendom*), apostolic letter, Vatican, June 20, 1894, https://www.papalencyclicals.net/leo13/l13praec.htm.

7. Arthur Weigall, *The Paganism in Our Christianity* (New York: G. P. Putnam's Sons, 1928), 145.

8. Ellen G. White, *The Great Controversy* (Nampa, ID: Pacific Press®, 2002), 592.

9. White, 607.

13

Ablaze With God's Glory

One of the more significant events of World War I was the sinking of the Cunard ocean liner RMS *Lusitania* on Friday, May 7, 1915. As Germany waged submarine warfare against the United Kingdom of Great Britain and Ireland, the British Royal Navy blockaded Germany. The *Lusitania* was identified and torpedoed by a German U-boat. It sank in eighteen minutes. The vessel went down eleven miles off the coast of Ireland, near Kinsale, killing 1,198 people and leaving 763 survivors. The sinking turned public opinion in many countries against Germany. It contributed to the American entry into World War I and became an iconic symbol in military recruiting campaigns as the reason the war was being fought.

A story associated with this disaster has relevance for Bible-believing Christians, especially for Seventh-day Adventists living in the last days of human history. Lord Joseph Duveen was the head of a prestigious art firm in the United States. In 1915, he planned to

send one of his experts to England to examine some ancient

pottery. He booked passage on the *Lusitania*. Then the German Embassy issued a warning that the liner might be torpedoed. Duveen wanted to call off the trip: "I can't take the risk of your being killed," he said to his young expert.

"Don't worry," the man replied, "I'm a strong swimmer, and when I read what was happening in the Atlantic, I began hardening myself by spending time every day in a tub of ice water. At first I could stand it only a few minutes, but this morning I stayed in that tub nearly two hours."

Naturally, Duveen laughed. It sounded preposterous. But his expert sailed; the *Lusitania* was torpedoed. The young man was rescued after nearly five hours in the chilly ocean, still in excellent condition.[1]

Just as this young man took the warnings seriously and prepared himself in advance for the tough times that were coming, so Jesus has given a message to prepare us for His soon return. The announcement of the three angels' messages to every man, woman, and child on this planet is specially designed by Christ to prepare each of us for His second coming.

These end-time messages are Heaven's last appeal to a dying planet. We ignore them at our own peril. They come to us from God's heart of divine love. To casually set them aside or treat them with careless indifference is to risk eternal loss.

In 1 Thessalonians 5:4–6, the apostle Paul writes, "But you, brethren, are not in darkness, so that this Day should overtake you as a thief. You are all sons of light and sons of the day. We are not of the night nor of darkness. Therefore let us not sleep, as others do, but let us watch and be sober."

Christ has given us these last-day messages so we can prepare for the momentous events soon to burst upon this world. These messages are of little use if we carelessly dismiss and ignore them. They are of little use if they do not radically change our lives.

Ellen White counsels us about the importance of preparing for the final events of Earth's history: "The end is very near. We who know the truth should be preparing for what is soon to break upon the world as an overwhelming surprise."[2] Prophecy predicts that there will be a mighty revival among God's people. They will enter into earnest prayer, repentance, confession, unity, and a commitment to completing God's work on Earth. Filled with the Spirit of God, they will go out with the Word of God in their hearts and Bibles in their hands to share the message of God's love.

Lighted with God's glory
At the end of time, Revelation 14 describes a worldwide church, spanning the globe with the good news of the eternal gospel. It reveals a last-day message, calling all men and women to "fear God and give glory to Him, for the hour of His judgment has come; and worship Him who made heaven and earth, the sea and springs of water" (verse 7).

In Revelation 18, a fourth angel joins the three angels of Revelation 14. This angel gives power to the proclamation of the three angels, and the earth is lighted with the glory of God. Revelation 18 focuses on the major events leading up to the climax of human history and the final, ultimate triumph of the gospel. Verses 1–6 describe what is coming in rather specific detail.

"After these things I saw another angel coming down from heaven, having great authority, and the earth was illuminated with his glory" (Revelation 18:1). The angel comes down from the glorious presence of God in the throne room of the sanctuary, commissioned to proclaim God's last message of mercy and warn the inhabitants of the earth of what is coming upon the planet.

The text says that the angel comes with "great authority." The New Testament Greek word for "authority" is *exousia*. Jesus uses this word in the Gospel of Matthew in connection with the sending out of His disciples. In Matthew 10:1, Jesus gives His disciples "authority" over the principalities and powers of hell. He sends them out with the divine power to be victorious in the battle between good and evil. In Matthew 28:18, 19, He again sends them out but this time with all authority in heaven and Earth to go and "make disciples of all the nations" (verse 19). Filled with the power of the Holy Spirit and going forth with the authority of the living Christ—who in His life and death triumphed over the principalities and powers of hell—the New Testament church lighted the earth with the glory of God. In a few short years, the disciples proclaimed the gospel in the then-known world (Colossians 1:23).

In the end time, the Holy Spirit will be poured out in unprecedented power, and the gospel will rapidly spread to the ends of the earth. Thousands will be converted in a day, and God's grace and truth will impact the entire planet.

If this is true—and it is—is it not wise for us to open our hearts to receive this mighty outpouring of the Spirit to finish the work of God on Earth? Is it not wise to ask Jesus to take anything out of our lives that would hinder this mighty outpouring of the Spirit? Is it not wise to seek God for the heart cleansing necessary to receive the latter rain of the Spirit in all His fullness?

Glory, honor, and power

Throughout Revelation, three important words are linked together: God's *glory*, God's *honor*, and God's *power*. Revelation 4:11 says, "You are worthy, O Lord, / To receive glory and honor and power." Consider Revelation 5:12: "Worthy is the Lamb who was slain / To receive power and riches and wisdom, / And strength and honor and glory and blessing!"

Notice the association between glory, honor, and power in Revelation 19:1: "Salvation and glory and honor and power belong to the Lord our God!" And notice how Revelation closes: "And they shall bring the glory and the honor of the nations into it [the New Jerusalem]" (Revelation 21:26).

The great controversy between good and evil in the universe is about God's honor—His reputation. Satan, a rebel angel, has declared that God is unjust—He demands worship but gives little in return. The evil one declares that God's law is arbitrary, restricting our freedom and limiting our joy. Jesus' life, death, and resurrection exploded that myth. The One who created us plunged into this snake pit of a world to redeem us. On the cross, He answered Satan's charges and demonstrated that God is both loving and just. Charmed by His love and concerned about His honor, His end-time people reveal His glory—His loving, self-sacrificing character—to a self-centered, godless world, and the earth is illuminated by the character of God.

Remember when Moses asked God to show him His glory? God responded to Moses, "I will make all My goodness pass before you" (Exodus 33:19). God's goodness is His character.

The earth will be filled with the glory of God when we are so completely overwhelmed with His love, when we so totally comprehend its depth and so fully grasp how amazing that grace is, that our characters are changed by His redeeming love.

As the apostle John declares in 1 John 3:1, 2: "Behold what manner of love the Father has bestowed on us, that we should be called children of God! . . . Beloved, now we are children of God; and it has not yet been revealed what we shall be, but we know that when He is revealed, we shall be like Him, for we shall see Him as He is."

Revealing His love in our personal lives reveals His glory and character to the world. Ellen White puts it this way: "The message of Christ's righteousness is to sound from one end of the earth to the other to prepare the way of the Lord. This is the glory of God, which closes the work of the third angel."[3] Babylon and all false religions speak of the glory of man. Genuine Christianity speaks of the glory of Christ. Babylon and all false religions speak of my reputation and my honor. Genuine Christianity speaks of Christ's reputation and Christ's honor. Babylon and all false religions speak of human works—what I have done. Genuine Christianity speaks of what Christ has done. Babylon and all false religions speak of what I am doing for Christ, not what He is doing for me.

Genuine Christianity

A Christian's testimony is simply this: Christ has done for me what I could not do for myself. Babylon and all false religions are based on distortions of biblical truth and founded on human opinion. Genuine Christianity is based on the truth as it is in Jesus, anchored in God's Word.

Gratitude for all Christ has done for us motivates our behavior and leads us to commit our lives to Him. The last message to be proclaimed to a world engulfed in spiritual darkness, carried by three angels in the midst of heaven, is "Fear God and give glory to Him" (Revelation 14:7). There is no glory in our work, no glory in our righteousness, and no glory in our goodness.

Ellen White states it plainly: "What is justification by faith? It is the work of God in laying the glory of man in the dust, and doing for man that which it is not in his power to do for himself."[4]

Where are we in the stream of time? Where are we in the panorama of last-day events? Where are we in the march of history? We are poised on the verge of a religious, political, and economic union. The accumulated figures of sin are rapidly reaching their limit in God's record book.

God is preparing a people to proclaim the marvels of His grace, the greatness of His love, the goodness of His character, the righteousness of His law, and the beauty of His truth. Bathed in His righteousness, they are justified by His grace and sanctified through His power. They love His truth, live His truth, and proclaim His truth. They count all things but loss for Christ. He is their all in all. They care not for earthly fame or human accolades. Position, prestige, and earthly praise mean little to them.

With the apostle Paul, they say, "For to me, to live is Christ" (Philippians 1:21). Empowered by His Spirit, they proclaim His love and share His grace. The earth is lighted with the glory—the character—of God. The Holy Spirit is poured out in latter rain power. Hearts are touched. Lives are changed. The world is reached, and Jesus comes again.

Christ's return makes all the difference

Many years ago, Lord Adelbert Cecil was converted to Christ, and his life was dramatically changed. He now had a burning passion for sharing the Christ who had done so much for him. His one desire was to preach the gospel. He traveled to North America and spent much of his time in Canada. He shared the love of Christ everywhere he went—in large cities, in remote villages, among farmers, in lumber camps, and in quiet seaside towns.

He told the story of one day passing the house of a man he knew was once a Christian but had seriously drifted away from Christ. He saw the man at his woodpile, industriously chopping wood for his cookstove. Knowing the man to be a backslider, one who had once been a faithful witness for his Savior but now was no longer attending church, Lord Cecil paused and shouted to him, "The Lord is coming, brother, the Lord is coming!" He said no more and continued walking. The warning "The Lord is coming!" burned its way into that man's soul. The words reached the core of his being.

Like a two-edged sword, they pierced his heart. His conscience smote him. They echoed again and again in his mind: *"The Lord is coming!"* It seemed he could not forget them. That urgent appeal from God's servant that the coming of the Lord was near so impressed the man that he recommitted his life to Christ and returned to church. Living in the light of the second coming of Christ is powerful and changes your life.[5]

An appeal

In the fading light of human history, in these critical times, in this crisis hour, I invite you to say, "Jesus, take away all human pride. Help me to trust in You and You alone. Make me what You want me to be, and keep me faithful until You come again."

In faith, you may proclaim, "Jesus, use me in this closing work to make a difference in our world. I do not want to play religious games. I am not interested in a superficial, powerless faith. Lord, I want to know You deeply, love You supremely, and share the message of Your soon return with the people around me. Lord, I sense, as never before, that You have an end-time message to proclaim to the entire world, and I choose to cooperate with You in giving this final warning message of Your soon coming so You can return in Your glory. Amen!"

1. Vernon C. Grounds, "Getting Into Shape Spiritually," *Christianity Today*, February 2, 1979, 25.

2. Ellen G. White, *Testimonies for the Church* (Mountain View, CA: Pacific Press®, 1948), 8:28.

3. Ellen G. White, *Testimonies for the Church* (Mountain View, CA: Pacific Press®, 1948), 6:19.

4. Ellen G. White, *Testimonies to Ministers and Gospel Workers* (Mountain View, CA: Pacific Press®, 1923), 456.

5. "Lord Cecil," Bible Truth, last accessed September 22, 2022, https://bibletruth publishers.com/lord-cecil/messages-of-gods-love-1966/la179044.